"I have been using the Messianic Daily Devotional since it was first published. I have found it to be a vital resource in my daily walk as a Jewish Believer. There are many devotionals out there, but few keep us grounded in the Messianic Walk every day. I highly recommend this devotional." –E.W.

"Words can't even begin to express how this devotional has touched the lives of our family. The daily messages go to your soul, and you know that Kevin and his family have most definitely been anointed for this work.... This book is a MUST HAVE for the serious student of not only the Word, but of your relationship to the Creator of all things and His Son, Yeshua. This devotional is not ear candy like many devotionals I have read before. There are no catchy phrases or one-liners, but serious reflections and gut-checks of who you are in Yeshua, and where you stand in your relationship with Elohim. You will want extra copies of this book to hand out... May ADONAI bless you and keep you as you spend time [in] devotion to Him!!" –A.L.

"I am on my second time through this wonderful devotional, and I find something new each day. It amazes me how well the devotional relates many of the passages to everyday life and the situations I face. While only a part of my devotional time, ADONAI adds to my study greatly through this devotional. This will be a great addition to your faith walk." –D.F.

"... I have read many devotionals, but none quite like this. I cannot help but give this book a five star rating. It was, without a doubt, one of the best devotionals that I have ever read.... I highly recommend this book to everyone, student and teacher alike." –J.K.

"This is my third year using this devotional. Each time, I use a different colored highlighter as new and different lessons are revealed to me. It has brought comfort, encouragement, provocation and more. I consider this devotional to be my most valuable biblical accessory." –J.M.

"I praise the Lord for this wonderful devotional. I am challenged and encouraged every day, and the prayers at the end are such a great jumping off point into my daily prayers. Thank you, Kevin Geoffrey, for sharing this with us." –M.J.

"I have never been so blessed. I look forward each day to reading what has been written [in the devotional]. My heart leaps with such excitement at the truths that are revealed. Once again, you have done an incredible job. Thank you!!!" –T.A.

"From the first page, we knew that there was something different about this devotional. It does not contain just nice thoughts, but reaches down into the very depths of your being asking you to 'come up here' to a new level of commitment. We will continue to share this devotional with others. Thank you!"
–D.F. & C.F.

MESSIANIC *Torah* DEVOTIONAL

KEVIN GEOFFREY

PERFECT *Word*
P · U · B · L · I · S · H · I · N · G

A ministry of Perfect Word Ministries

A ministry of Perfect Word Ministries

PO Box 82954 • Phoenix, AZ 85071
www.PerfectWordMinistries.com
1-888-321-PWMI

ISBN #: 0-9785504-4-7

שְׁמַע יִשְׂרָאֵל יהוה אֱלֹהֵינוּ יהוה אֶחָד
וְאָהַבְתָּ אֵת יהוה אֱלֹהֶיךָ בְּכָל־לְבָבְךָ
וּבְכָל־נַפְשְׁךָ וּבְכָל־מְאֹדֶךָ וְהָיוּ הַדְּבָרִים הָאֵלֶּה
אֲשֶׁר אָנֹכִי מְצַוְּךָ הַיּוֹם עַל־לְבָבֶךָ

"Hear, O Yis'rael, ADONAI our God, ADONAI is
one. And you will love ADONAI your God with all
your heart, and with all your soul, and with all
your might. And these words which I am
commanding you today will be on your heart."

דְּבָרִים D'variym (Deuteronomy) 6:4-6

Table of Contents

Preface

The Torah tells the story of a people specially selected by God, set apart from all the nations of the earth to be a servant and a blessing. To me, this is both a joyful and a heart-rending story: joyful, because God chose tiny, insignificant Israel; yet heart-rending, because Israel would not—and has not yet—embraced her selection. As a Jew, I equally rejoice and lament over the account of the beginnings of my people, but I also see a present and a future hope for us all through the Torah's fulfillment and aim, the Messiah Yeshua. It is with conflicted feelings, then, that I offer you the *Messianic Torah Devotional*—the reflections of a Jew who loves his people and his Messiah, and desires to see them reconciled to each other once and for all.

During the preparation of this volume, I experienced the Torah in a way that was surprisingly different from all my previous encounters with it. Since the Torah is built on a framework chronicling Israel's birth and foundational journey with God, I often felt as though I were participating with Israel on her quest—benefiting spiritually from the reports of both her victories and her mistakes, and learning in a fundamental way how ADONAI loves and treats His own. But to my dismay, there were also many instances in which I felt like an imprisoned, silent observer—able to neither encourage nor warn Israel concerning the inevitable events awaiting her on the ensuing pages of Scripture. The result was a radically moving experience—one that has reaffirmed my convictions and passion for every Jew to return to God's Torah and the covenantal calling and responsibility that goes with it.

"Torah" is a heavy-weight subject in the Messianic arena, and many of us have our own preconceptions about how it should be approached. I must therefore make it clear that one thing I did *not* intend to accomplish with this book was to create a resource to aid in the study and application of Torah commands. In writing the *Messianic Torah Devotional*, I sought only to unveil the Torah as a devotional source for the disciple of Messiah—to see if its teachings would lead us to study our *hearts* and seek more fervently after God. To that end, each devotional is not always about the main point—or perhaps even the *best* point—of a given portion of Scripture. The point they *do* make is the one I felt *inspired* to deliver—you may judge for yourself if the Lord had a hand in my decisions or my conclusions.

Thank you for allowing me to walk with you through the Torah as we continue to follow closely in the footsteps of our Master. As you make this book part of your daily devotions to God, I pray that the Scriptures contained herein will captivate and draw you; that their corresponding devotional writings will spark in you a fresh understanding of the Scriptures; and that as you begin to pray in accordance with the Word of God, the Spirit will lead you into a time of deep and meaningful devotion, worship and praise that will change your life—today, forever, and for good.

In Yeshua,

Kevin Geoffrey
August 18, 2008

Introduction

The *Messianic Torah Devotional* is the second companion volume to the immensely well-received *Messianic Daily Devotional*, published in 2006. Continuing in the tradition of its predecessors, the *Messianic Torah Devotional* offers insightful, challenging, Scripture-based devotional writings with a unique, but distinctly Messianic Jewish point of view.

As noted in our previous books, these devotionals are not designed to be sources for learning about Messianic Jewish theology. Though the subject matter for this *particular* book did occasionally warrant some explanation within the devotionals themselves, we nevertheless purposed to avoid a teaching style intended to impart *information*, and instead opted for a personal style designed to encourage *devotion*. Time and again, this approach has been affirmed by our readers, as they consistently comment that our devotionals are like none they have ever read before.

Unlike the *Messianic Daily Devotional*, which covers many different topics related to our daily walk with Messiah, the *Messianic Torah Devotional* has a very specific focus: Genesis through Deuteronomy—also collectively known as *the Torah*. Though the five books of Moses contain universally relevant material, at their core is the covenant ADONAI made with the sons of Israel—thus establishing the Torah as the distinctive, foundational document for the Jewish people. The *Messianic Torah Devotional* was written—and is therefore best understood—in light of this dynamic.

The Devotional Nature of the Torah

Though the Torah outwardly appears to be central to the more religious forms of today's Judaisms, it is generally perceived by Jews and Christians alike as archaic and irrelevant to contemporary life. But despite its allegedly obsolete rules and regulations, Scripture itself testifies to the devotional nature of the Torah. Indeed, Israel is to have Torah's *"words... on your heart,"*[1] and King David says that Torah is the happy man's *"delight, and in [ADONAI's] Torah he will meditate by day and by night."*[2] For the Jew, this should be an inescapable reality—that the Torah *"is not an empty thing for you, for it is your life, and by this thing you [will] prolong [your] days...."*[3]

Contrary to popular belief, the Torah remains in force as the covenant of national distinction for the Jewish people—including and *especially* Jewish believers in the Messiah Yeshua, or Messianic Jews. It should go without saying that the inauguration and reality of the New Covenant[4] has not rendered the covenant of Torah inoperative, since the Master Himself maintains *"that until the heaven and the earth may pass away, not one yud (ﬧ) or one stroke may pass away from the Torah...."*[5] As the covenant of national distinction, the Torah holds the key to our identity as both Messianics and Jews, therefore deserving our attention as a devotional source as well as the founding text of our faith.

Though the Torah—indeed, the whole of the Hebrew Scriptures—is a uniquely Jewish text, we would be remiss in failing to mention that *"all Scripture is*

---

[1] Deuteronomy 6:6
[2] Psalm 1:2
[3] Deuteronomy 32:47
[4] Jeremiah 31:31, Luke 22:20
[5] Matthew 5:18; cf. Hebrews 7:11ff

God-breathed, and profitable for teaching, for reproof, for setting aright, for instruction that is in righteousness, that the man of God may be complete, equipped for every good work."[6] As Scripture, surely *"the Torah is good"*[7] for all believers in Yeshua, regardless of heritage or ethnicity—though the way we practically apply it may differ. It is on the basis of this reality, therefore, that we offer the *Messianic Torah Devotional* gladly and equally to all disciples of the Messiah Yeshua.

Utilizing the Traditional Reading Cycle

It was clear from the beginning that it would be insufficient to tackle the Torah haphazardly, choosing passages for devotional treatment according to a somewhat arbitrary standard. How many devotionals, for example, would such a book contain? How would we overcome the tendency to focus on overtly spiritual selections above those that are seemingly mundane? Would we gloss over whole sections of Scripture just because they contain unpleasant or discomforting content? If the devotionals were to collectively represent the Torah as a whole, we needed a more rigid, systematic outline—and Judaism's annual Torah reading cycle was the immediately obvious solution.[8] By locking ourselves into the traditional framework, it solved the problem of what and how much to write. Within the confines of its fifty-four divisions of roughly equal length, we could freely string together our devotional subjects, while leaving no portion of Torah unturned.

The challenge created by this restricted approach, however, was that the devotionals could no longer be based on isolated passages of Scripture (as they are in

---

[6] 2Timothy 3:16-17
[7] 1Timothy 1:8
[8] See Appendix A on page 181 for more about the reading cycle.

our other devotional books). Instead, they had to be written in the context of much larger portions—often several chapters that naturally cover a great deal of Scriptural ground. Opting for this structure, then, meant that we would be trying to capture the essence of an entire Torah portion in a single devotional. While three pages of text can hardly do justice to an entire portion of Scripture, each devotional is nevertheless based on at least two if not three Scripture passages, selected for their inspirational qualities as well as their thematic continuity with one another. We believe this approach has allowed us to adequately characterize each portion, while granting us the flexibility to explore its more devotional qualities.

Other Features

Though the Torah devotionals follow a modified and extended format from that of our other devotional books, the writings themselves remain neither teachings nor commentaries on the passages of Scripture, but exhortations that are intended to encourage discipleship and devotion to God. Also unlike our other devotional offerings, we encourage you to read the entire Torah portion *before* considering its corresponding devotional. This will not only put the devotional into its fullest context, but will hopefully enhance your devotional response to the Word.

Each devotional is named for its corresponding Torah portion, as so indicated on its opening page—first the *transliterated*[9] Hebrew, then the actual Hebrew, followed by the English *translation*.[10] Beneath the translation you will find the full Scripture reference for

---

[9] A transliteration is a phonetic representation of words from another language, i.e., "Yeshua" is an English transliteration of יֵשׁוּעַ.
[10] A translation gives the *meaning* of a word, while transliteration gives only its *pronunciation*.

the entire Torah portion. Occasionally, you will also see verse numbers set off by parenthesis, indicating alternate verse numberings as found in Jewish Bibles. The devotional concludes with a suggested prayer that will help give you a "jump-start" as you enter into a deeper time of fellowship with ADONAI.

One of the most unique features of the *Messianic Torah Devotional* is that many of the devotionals contain "restored" Hebrew names and places—the most obvious of which are Yeshua (rendered in most English translations of the Bible as "Jesus"), and Messiah (rendered in most English translations as "Christ"). This "restoration" was done for several reasons. First, it serves as a reminder of the Hebraic nature of our Scriptures—and how often they can be truly foreign to our western-thinking minds. Second, it demonstrates the ongoing and perpetual Jewishness of our faith and our Messiah. Finally, it helps to increase our familiarity with and love for the Hebrew language—the native tongue of the nation of Israel, and of her promised redeemer, Yeshua.

Not wishing to trivialize the use of Hebrew within a book written for an English-speaking audience, we have gone a step beyond simply embedding transliterated Hebrew. In passages of Scripture that were originally written in Hebrew, we have also included the actual Hebrew letters with their *nikudot* (vowel marks or vowel points).[11] This should be especially beneficial for those who are just beginning to learn the Hebrew language. In some cases, we have included the translated English word just after the restored Hebrew and transliteration. Additionally, a reverse glossary— alphabetized according to the transliterated English—

_____

[11] Most of the vowel sounds in Hebrew are not represented by letters of the *alef-beit*, but instead have been preserved for posterity through the vowel-pointing system of the *nikudot*.

has been provided on page 175, so that the reader may look up the meaning of each Hebrew word used in the devotionals.

The Sacred Name

For the sake of brevity, there are two familiar Hebrew words used throughout the devotionals that are rendered with transliteration *alone*—Yeshua and Adonai.[12] However, when the word "ADONAI" is printed with all capital letters, it actually represents a *different* word altogether: יהוה, the "Sacred Name" of God.[13]

So why don't we use an English transliteration to help us pronounce the Sacred Name? The reason is that we simply do not know how to properly pronounce it. According to Jewish tradition, the Name is not to be spoken, out of proper respect for the Holy One. Whenever the Scriptures were read aloud, the reader would say "Adonai," rather than uttering the Name itself. Thus, when the Jewish scribes were adding the *nikudot* to the Scriptures, they purposely superimposed the *nikudot* for אֲדֹנָי, *Adonai* upon the Name in order to remind the reader to make the appropriate substitution. With time, the pronunciation of the Name was lost—or at least obscured beyond recovery.

Though some scholars and other individuals maintain that the pronunciation of the Name has indeed been preserved from antiquity—or can be reasonably discerned from what we know of Hebrew—it is *our* belief that this is just not so. Therefore, with no confidence in the accuracy of any given pronunciation,

---

[12] A title for God, meaning Lord or Master.
[13] In English, this name is sometimes represented as YHWH or YHVH, the English letters which correspond to the four Hebrew letters of The Name.

we have opted to represent יהוה with "ADONAI," in keeping with the tradition. Where יהוה appears next to אֲדֹנָי, *Adonai* in the text, the name that is rendered with capital letters is the one used to represent the Sacred Name, i.e. *Adonai 'ELOHIYM*.[14]

Young's Literal Translation of the Holy Bible (1862/1898) by J.N. Young

One of the challenges in devotional writing—or any kind of Bible teaching, for that matter—is avoiding personal "inspiration" or "revelation" sparked solely from the English translation. When a teacher relies exclusively on a specific translation, he risks having a distorted view of the text, or even missing its point altogether.

Although translators do their best to retain the meanings of the original text, there is always some linguistic work and paraphrasing based on the translator's understanding. While some Bible translations take more liberty than others, their goal is generally to make the Scriptures more readable for the new audience—and a translation that is more readable is therefore more meaningful. While this approach is helpful in communicating ideas and concepts, such alterations unavoidably add to or change the meaning of a passage when it is read subjectively.

In an attempt to compensate for the skewed "inspiration" that can come from reading English translations, we chose to work with the *Young's Literal Translation*. First published in 1862, this "literal" translation attempts to retain direct one-to-one word

---

[14] The Hebrew, אֱלֹהִים, *'Elohiym*, and occasionally אֵל, *El*, is usually translated in English as "God." Where you see the word "God" in the devotional Scripture passages originally written in Hebrew, it is translating this word.

translations, word order, colloquialisms, and literal phrase renderings from the original language. As you can imagine, this makes for a sometimes dramatically different reading from other English translations. Despite its advantages, however, the "old English" style of the text can be quite cumbersome, often making it difficult to easily understand.

Thankfully, another aspect of the *Young's* worked in our favor—the translation is in the public domain, and therefore free from copyright. As such, we had the freedom to work with the text, bringing the language into 21st century North American English. We were also able to restore the Hebrew names of people and places, along with other words which we felt worked better in the original language. As we made these updates, we were constantly forced to go back to the original languages, as well as making comparisons with various other English translations. In the end, we arrived at a fresh, meaningful, and hopefully accurate translation.

Although every attempt was made to keep the translation as literal as possible, there were some instances where additional English words were necessary. Where Young added words not in the original language, they are set off from the italicized Scriptures as normal text. Where *we* added words that were neither in the *Young's* nor in the original text, they are set off by brackets. These words were added to make for a smooth, unencumbered reading of the passage— but in most cases, you will find that they can be read and understood without our bracketed embellishments.

The Daily Discipline of Devotion

Each of us is in a different stage of life, with varying responsibilities, pressures, and other demands on our time and energy. As disciples of Messiah, however, we cannot afford to allow *life* to dictate how we *live*. The only way we can ever hope to gain control over our lives is to yield ourselves completely to God. Though we may prefer it to be otherwise, such surrender is not a one-time event—it is ongoing, and requires a daily commitment. Undying devotion to God is key to living an effective, useful, *and happy* life for Messiah.

One way to begin developing that daily discipline of devotion is through the use of devotional resources such as the *Messianic Daily Devotional,* the *Messianic Mo'adiym Devotional,* and the *Messianic Torah Devotional.* Though you may find the writings to be inspirational and useful for sharpening you as a believer in Yeshua, these books are only intended to be a starting place for what we pray will be a meaningful and ever-deepening devotional life.

The following are just a few practical suggestions for how to incorporate the *Messianic Torah Devotional* into your life, as you continually develop that daily discipline of devotion.

Examples of Ways to Use the Devotional Book

❖ In private devotions—to grow in your relationship with ADONAI as you delight in His Torah

❖ In public meetings—as a devotional complement to the weekly Torah reading

❖ During family devotions—to begin a time of prayer, discussion, or study

❖ As a discipleship tool—to help new believers get into the Word and allow ADONAI to transform their lives

❖ Between accountability partners—to read together or apart, in order to discuss or share insights that will strengthen you both as disciples of Messiah

Goals to Consider for Your Torah Devotions

❖ Set aside special time regularly to be alone with God—congregational meetings and Torah studies are wonderful, but they should never take the place of our personal time with Him.

❖ Read a devotional according to the schedule you establish, but don't forget the Scriptures! Remember, each set of devotional Scriptures is excerpted from a larger Torah portion. These particular devotionals are meant to be read *following* your reading of the Word.

❖ Pray! Rather than *concluding* your devotional time with the prayers we have provided, use them to jump-start your time with ADONAI.

❖ Consider ways to extend your devotional time— for example, put on your favorite praise and worship CD and see what happens!

This is *devotion*: to devote ourselves fully to our God, to give our lives over to Him completely, and to be captivated by the gravity and grace of His presence, so that *"in Him, we [will] live, and move, and be…"*[15]

---

[15] Acts 17:28

MESSIANIC
Torah
DEVOTIONAL

בראשית

B'reshiyt · Genesis

בראשית

In the Beginning
בְּרֵאשִׁית **B'reshiyt (Genesis) 1:1-6:8**

*"In the beginning, God shaped the heavens
and the earth—the earth being nothingness and
emptiness, with darkness on the face of the deep
and* רוּחַ אֱלֹהִים, *Ruach 'Elohiym fluttering on the
face of the waters—and God said, 'Let light be,'
and light was."* בְּרֵאשִׁית *B'reshiyt 1:1-3*

In the beginning—from the very shaping of the
heavens and the earth—was the Word. And the Word
was with God, and the Word was God. Without Him,
not even one thing existed, for it was through Him that
"God said…" and all things came into being. Into the
nothingness the Word was spoken… and in the
beginning, the nothingness heard and obeyed.

For six days, God labored over the creation of all
things, yet His work consisted of but a single, simple
act, *"and God said…"* Emptiness gave way to substance;
darkness gave way to light. The nothingness replied to
the Word—yielding to His command; responding to
the authority of His will. And yet, Creation faltered…
in us. When *we* heard the Word, substance became
nothingness; light reverted to darkness. Why, when it is

so clear that even *nothing* can hear, do we fail to *listen* to the Word and *do* what He *says*?

> *"Now the serpent was sly—more than every beast of the field which* יהוה אֱלֹהִים, ADONAI *'Elohiym had made. And [the serpent] said to the woman, 'Did God really say, "Do not eat of every tree of the garden?"''"* בְּרֵאשִׁית B'reshiyt 3:1

"Did God really say...?" It's the question of every curious mind and the assertion of every rebellious heart. ADONAI 'Elohiym had spoken Creation into existence through His Word, only to have doubt immediately cast upon Him. With one simple question, the Creator's authority was undermined and His sovereignty tested: *"Did God really say...?"*

Did God really say not to eat of the tree of knowledge of good and evil? Did God really say that the man and woman would die if they did? Whether we are being seduced by a snake or questioning our own convictions, it always comes back to one thing: *"Did God really say...?"* Though our hearts and minds may defiantly pose the question, what's most important is that we get the right answer—and that we trust that it is true, despite the lies we might otherwise believe.

> *"And* ADONAI *said to* קַיִן, *Kayin, 'Why are you [burning with] anger? And why has your countenance fallen? Is there not—if you do [what is] right—acceptance? But if you do not [do what is] right, sin is crouching at the entryway—and for you [is] its desire, but you [must] rule over it.'"* בְּרֵאשִׁית B'reshiyt 4:6-7

When we hear the Word, we have a choice: to listen, or to ignore. If we pay no heed to His Word, separation from God is inevitable (cf. 4:16). But here is the Good News: though sin is in the world—*"crouching at the entryway,"* waiting around the corner, sneaking up from behind—the righteousness we have in God grants us rulership over that which desires to enslave us. By the power of the Word of God, we confidently stand tall over cowering, stealthy sin.

In the beginning, *"God said,"* and the Word of God spoke forth life into Creation. Though sin challenges the Word, we must rule over it—and we are able to do so because we have been created anew. We have been given life again by the living Word of God—our Master, the Messiah Yeshua. As new creations in *His* image, let us turn from the darkness and nothingness that we are without Him. May we hear and obey the Word that He really and truly did say....

෨ ๙

ADONAI, God, remind me of my beginnings. Make me remember what it was like when I first came to know You—how You created light in me where there formerly had been nothing but darkness. Deliver me forever, Lord, from the sin that is still crouching in the corners of my life, and then take me back to the day when You redeemed me—recreated me—and made me clean by the washing of the water by the Word. Thank You, O God, for always allowing me to be renewed—to find my new beginning forever in You....

Noach

נח

Noah
בְּרֵאשִׁית B'reshiyt (Genesis) 6:9-11:32

"נֹחַ, Noach was a righteous man; whole[-hearted] he had been among his generation. With God did נֹחַ, Noach walk...." בְּרֵאשִׁית B'reshiyt 6:9

Noach enters history with no announcement or warning—he was simply a righteous man. Perhaps there were others of Noach's generation who could have also been considered righteous... at least by some arbitrary standard of "goodness." And yet there was one thing that set Noach apart from everyone else of his day: He was *whole-hearted*, so that *"with God did Noach walk."*

So many of us spend our lives seeking and searching for something to make us complete—anything that will give us meaning and purpose in our lives. But Noach was *whole* in *heart* because he filled himself with the only thing that can truly complete a man: God. When we look to the world to fill us up, we really do walk alone; but the one who is wholehearted in the ways of righteousness will always walk with God.

"And God said [to Noach], 'This is the sign of the covenant which I am giving between Me and

*you and every living creature that is with you, to
[all] generations forever: I will put My rainbow in
the clouds, and it will be for the sign of the covenant
between Me and the earth. And it will come to
pass... that the rainbow will be seen in the cloud,
and I will remember My covenant—which is
between Me and you and every living creature
among all living things—and the waters [will]
never again become a deluge to destroy all living
things. And [when] the rainbow is in the cloud,
and I see it, [it will cause Me] to remember the
covenant forever between God and every living
creature among all living things which are on the
earth.'"* בְּרֵאשִׁית *B'reshiyt 9:12-16*

When we walk righteously with God, we offer Him
trustworthy service. ADONAI honored such righteousness
in Noach by making him the representative recipient of
His eternal covenant with all living things. Expecting
His covenant to be kept, ADONAI sealed it with a sign, so
that *both* of us—He and all the descendants of Noach—
would remain faithful and remember His promises
forever.

And yet we forget, giving ADONAI countless reasons
to nullify His promises. Thankfully, He doesn't... and
though we fail to honor our end of the contract, ADONAI
goes on, continuing to remember and refusing to go
back on His Word. Though the Lord brings rain and
clouds to cover the earth, their parting reveals a sign in
the heavens to remind the Creator that even while the
sky is breaking, *His* promises may *never* be broken.

*"And they said, 'Come, let us build for ourselves
a city and tower, and its head [will reach high] in
the heavens—and [let us] make for ourselves a*

name, lest we be scattered over the face of all the earth.'" בְּרֵאשִׁית *B'reshiyt 11:4*

In the face of ADONAI's faithfulness, we flaunt our strength in arrogance. Instead of remembering the promises of God, we bury them at our feet and erect monuments to ourselves upon them. But the plans of the unrighteous prophesy their own destruction. "We will go high, so that we will not be scattered." Our lives will fall apart. "We will stay low to avoid being seen." Our deeds will be exposed. "We will be our own gods, so that we will always be in control." We will lose command of everything we ever wanted to rule.

Yet for the righteous in each generation, ADONAI our God has a purpose. We do not need to build up our own cities, for God is the builder and destroyer of kingdoms—and *His* plan will bring us to *His* heights by *His* strength, power and might. If we hope to walk with God and to be called "righteous" by Him, it will be according to *His plan*, and not by *our choice*. Our desire, then, should be a life of devotion to God—not satisfying our own wants or walking pridefully in a strength not our own, but seeking after God to fill us up and make us whole… in heart…

∾ ❧

Father, You alone can make a man righteous—let me be one who walks only with You. Break me, my Master, that I will always be broken for Your service—never building my own kingdom by my own will, but working with You according to Your glorious plans. Thank You, Lord, for raising up the righteous ones for Yourself in every generation—I praise You, ADONAI, for You remember Your covenant with me forever. Remind me of Your promises and keep me holy, O God, that I may partake in the awesome blessings of life reserved for those who walk righteously with You.

Lech-L'cha

לֶךְ-לְךָ

Get Yourself Away
בְּרֵאשִׁית B'reshiyt (Genesis) 12:1-17:27

*"And ADONAI said to אַבְרָם, Av'ram, 'Get
yourself away from your land, and from your
relatives, and from the house of your father, into
the land which I [will] show you. And I [will]
make you become a great nation, and bless you,
and make your name great; and you [will] be a
blessing. And I [will] bless those who bless you,
and him who despises you I [will] curse, and
blessed in you will be all [the] families of the
ground [of the earth].'" בְּרֵאשִׁית B'reshiyt 12:1-3*

The covenant ADONAI begins to forge with Av'ram
is filled with promises of blessing: a great nation, a great
name, blessings for friend, and curses for foe. But did
Av'ram leave his homeland and his people behind merely
for the prospect of abundant blessing? What motivated
him to embark on such a journey with only the nebulous
assurances of a God he barely knew?

Perhaps Av'ram responded to ADONAI out of pure
faith. Maybe he acted out of strict obedience. In fact,
Av'ram's response to ADONAI was according to both
faith *and* obedience—any other reaction to the Father is
incomplete. Whether we hear His commands or abide

in His promises, our response must always be the same—
faith *and* obedience will unfailingly lead us anywhere the
Lord wants us to go.

> *"...the word of* ADONAI *came to* אַבְרָם, *Av'ram*
> *in a vision, saying, 'Fear not,* אַבְרָם, *Av'ram, I am*
> *a shield to you; your reward is exceedingly great.'*
> *...And* אַבְרָם, *Av'ram said, 'Behold, to me You have*
> *not given [any] offspring...' And [ADONAI] brought*
> *[Av'ram] outside, and said, 'Look attentively now*
> *toward the heavens and count the stars—if you*
> *are able to count them.' And He said to him, '[As*
> *many as] this is your offspring.' And [Av'ram]*
> *believed in* ADONAI, *and He credited it to him—*
> *righteousness."* בְּרֵאשִׁית *B'reshiyt 15:1-6*

As it often happens with many of us, time had
eroded Av'ram's faith. Without the ever-present voice
of affirmation, the void left Av'ram vulnerable to faith's
unrelenting nemesis: *fear*. Though faith had set Av'ram
on the path that would change his life forever, fear was
leading him into doubt: "Will ADONAI be faithful to
His promises? What has become of His covenant?"

Angst is overcome by the Word, which says, *"Fear
not... I am a shield to you."* When fear gets the better of
us and we turn to accuse God of not following through
on His promises, the Word tells us to *"look attentively"*
at the evidence of His sovereignty. When we trust
ADONAI—not because of where we *are*, but solely
because of who He *is*—our belief will triumph over fear,
and our trust will be credited to us as righteousness.

> *"...ADONAI appeared to* אַבְרָם, *Av'ram and*
> *said to him,* אֲנִי־אֵל שַׁדַּי, *aniy-El Shadai (I am God*
> *Almighty)—walk habitually before Me, and be*

perfect.... This is My covenant which you [must] keep...: every male of your [offspring] is to be circumcised... [in] the flesh of your foreskin, and it will be a sign of the covenant between Me and you.'" בְּרֵאשִׁית *B'reshiyt 17:1-11*

When we are far from the Lord, sometimes it is not fear that is our worst enemy, but forgetfulness. In this frame of mind, we seek solutions in our own strength, and the promises of God are absorbed into oblivion. This is how ADONAI found Av'ram in his ninety-ninth year: father of a teenage son, yet childless with regard to the covenant.

Our father Av'raham received the mark of circumcision as a reminder to never forget the covenant ADONAI made with him and his descendants. Faith and obedience will always be under attack by forces bent on derailing us from our destiny. So, at the place that our faith always fails—in our flesh—ADONAI marked us for Himself. It is a sign between ADONAI and the children of Yis'rael forever, saying, *"'walk habitually before Me...'* obey, have faith, and remember...."

৵৹ ৵৵

ADONAI, God of Av'raham, through faith and obedience do I *"get [myself] away"* from my former life and into *"the land which [You will] show [me]."* I praise You, for You are my shield—You never fail to restore my faith even when fear and doubt overwhelm me. Thank You, Lord, for calling and marking me as Your own, that I may be the beneficiary of the covenant You made with my father Av'raham. I bless Your Name, ADONAI, for You are forever faithful to remember Your promises—even when I continually and habitually forget...

וירא

And He Appeared
בְּרֵאשִׁית B'reshiyt (Genesis) 18:1-22:24

"And שָׂרָה, Sarah laughed in her heart, saying,
'After I have become old [how] will I have [this]
pleasure!?!?—my husband also is old!' And
ADONAI said to אַבְרָהָם, Av'raham, 'Why is this?
Sarah has laughed, saying, "Is it really true—[that]
I [will] bear [a child]—[even though] I am aged?"
Is anything too extraordinary for ADONAI?'"
בְּרֵאשִׁית B'reshiyt 18:12-14a

In this ordinary life, we are born and we grow—but
eventually, vitality begins to fade. As surely as the sun
rises and sets, so we will become old, growing feeble and
infirmed... the days of our youth nothing but a distant
memory. This is our lot in life, we think, and no force
on earth can alter this reality. The laws of nature set in
motion at the founding of the world cannot be changed—
and so we laugh away all but the inevitable.

But "is anything too extraordinary for ADONAI?"
Cannot the Creator of time suspend it, if it is His will?
Cannot He stop the sun in mid-air should He so choose?
So, too, can the God of the universe not only restore us
to health, but truly reverse the course of our lives. There
is nothing beyond His grasp, and His love for us is

without bounds. Can we not trust ADONAI to do all that He promises—and more… even that which, to us, seems *extraordinary?*

> *"Far be it from You to do according to this thing: to put to death the righteous with the wicked, [such] that it will be [the same for] the righteous as [for] the wicked. Far be it from You. Will the Judge of all the earth not do justice?"* בְּרֵאשִׁית *B'reshiyt 18:25*

When we are not doubting the Creator's ability to perform surpassingly great feats on our behalf, we can usually be found holding Him to our own double-standards. We tend to place very high expectations on the Lord, impatiently waiting for His swift justice to be poured out upon the wicked… especially upon those whom *we* determine to be in need of judgment…

…but *"far be it from"* Him to be the Judge of *us.*

Like Av'raham, we boldly reason with the Lord, though *we* ask for mercy because we have deemed *ourselves* worthy. But in the end, ADONAI alone will be the Judge of the righteous and the wicked alike. Will some who consider themselves righteous suffer the same fate as the wicked? *"Far be it from"* us to judge for ourselves; instead, let us endeavor only to do righteousness, allowing ADONAI Himself to *"do justice."*

> *"*יִצְחָק, *Yitz'chak spoke to* אַבְרָהָם, *Av'raham his father and said, 'My father,' and he said, 'Here am I, my son.' And he said, 'I see the fire and the wood, but where [is] the lamb for the burnt-offering?' And Av'raham said, 'God will provide*

> *for Himself the lamb for the burnt-offering, my*
> *son;' and they went on both of them together."*
> בְּרֵאשִׁית *B'reshiyt 22:7-8*

What kind of father would sacrifice his beloved son?
Surely, justice cannot be served by putting an innocent
man to death by his own father's hand. And yet, the
Lord requires it of His righteous servant, Av'raham.
There must be a reason for this insanity! What value
could there possibly be in carrying out such a command?

So that *"God will provide for Himself the lamb…"*

Yitz'chak represented all that Av'raham had to gain…
and to lose. Was Av'raham willing to put his trust fully
in God? Are we? Indeed, He alone is worthy of our
trust—not only because He rightly judges the righteous
and the wicked, but because He also offers *mercy* in
place of *sacrifice*. Though it was required of Av'raham
that blood must be spilled, God Himself provided the
lamb… and both justice and mercy were satisfied.

What kind of Father would sacrifice His beloved
Son? The kind who generously extends to us His
unsurpassing mercy every day. *"Is anything too
extraordinary for ADONAI?"*

∞ ∞

ADONAI, my God—You are extraordinary! I trust
You with my whole life, that You will show me mercy as
surely as You will dispense Your justice. I praise You,
Lord, for Your provision is always more than I could
ask or hope for… truly, You are extraordinary in all
Your ways. Thank You, Abba, for the sacrifice of Your
beloved Son—for providing the Lamb in my place. I
bless Your Name, ADONAI—holy, Extraordinary One!

חיי שרה

Sarah's Life
בְּרֵאשִׁית B'reshiyt (Genesis) 23:1-25:18

"And [the servant] said, 'ADONAI, God of my master אַבְרָהָם, Av'raham, cause [me] to meet— please—before me this day (and show grace to my master אַבְרָהָם, Av'raham; behold, I am standing by the fountain of water, and daughters of the men of the city are coming out to draw water. And may it be, [that] the young woman to whom I say, "Please, hold out your pitcher, that I [may] drink," and she says, "Drink, and I [will] water your camels also"), her You have decided for Your servant, for יִצְחָק, Yitz'chak; and by it I [will] know....'" בְּרֵאשִׁית *B'reshiyt 24:12-14*

We tend to play games with God, don't we? Sometimes, we treat Him like a magic eight-ball, shaking Him around until we get the answer we want. We think that by mixing our circumstances together with our prayers, the Lord will somehow give us a sign through it—something to hang our hopes on—because otherwise, we just can't seem to hear Him.

So, how do we account for the servant of Av'raham? Surely, he concocted this scenario to figure out how to choose Yitz'chak's wife... or did he? *"He is sending His messenger before you, and you will take a wife for my son from there." (24:7)*

There's a big difference between grasping for direction in random occurrences or self-fulfilling prophesies, and truly being directed by the Lord. He can and does guide us by giving us specific signs to follow. The question is, do we know ADONAI well enough to recognize His signs when we see them?

> *"And it came to pass, before he had finished speaking [to his heart], that... רִבְקָה, Riv'kah... came out, with her pitcher on her shoulder...."* בְּרֵאשִׁית *B'reshiyt 24:15*

Following a sign from God is certainly important, but how can we tell the difference between the guidance of the Lord and our own wishful thinking? In the case of Av'raham's servant, it was easy: even *before* He had finished entreating the Lord, his prayers were answered!

We can miss the signs and direction of the Lord for many reasons, but the most likely culprit is that we have already made up our minds about the way we think things should go. Perhaps we ought to give God a chance to show us *His* way first—*just in case* He has a better idea.

When we ask God for direction in our life and it seems like our prayers aren't even being heard, let us remember how easy it was for the servant of Av'raham. Maybe the reason we have so much trouble discerning answers from the Lord is that we're praying with pre-laid plans in our head. Isn't it possible that the Creator of the universe just might have something else in mind?

> *"And the man bowed [down] and worshipped ADONAI, and said, 'Blessed is ADONAI, God of my*

master אַבְרָהָם, Av'raham, who has not forsaken
His loving-kindness and His faithfulness toward
my master...." בְּרֵאשִׁית B'reshiyt 24:26-27b

When our prayers appear to go unanswered, we're
often quick to complain. But what about the times
when God answers clearly—how swift are we to bless
Him with worship, thanksgiving and praise? Aren't we
more likely to forget the Lord until the next time we
want something from Him? To a God who provides for
our every need, that's really not much of a blessing.

Answered prayer is one way that ADONAI shows *"His
loving-kindness and His faithfulness toward"* us. It proves
that He not only remembers us, but that He cares
enough about our daily needs to be both the compass
and destination on this journey we call Life.

So, when ADONAI responds to our requests, let us
not forget to be faithful to Him in return. Surely,
bowing down in worship and glorifying Him with
praise isn't giving too much of a blessing to a God who
answers prayer....

ॐ ॐ

ADONAI, I bless Your Name—You are glorious and
worthy of my worship. Teach me, Father, to run to You
in prayer when I am in need, and to not forget You when
You show Yourself faithful. Make me Your servant,
ADONAI, that by signs I may know Your ways—that I
will not set my mind according to my own desires, but
clearly see Your hand of loving-kindness. I speak to my
heart right now, Father, "Show me Your ways, that I
may follow You all of my days...."

תולדת

Genealogies
בְּרֵאשִׁית B'reshiyt (Genesis) 25:19-28:9

"'Let me eat, please!' עֵשָׂו, Esav said to יַעֲקֹב, Ya'akov.... And יַעֲקֹב, Ya'akov said, 'Sell today your birthright to me.' And עֵשָׂו, Esav said, 'Look, I am going to die, and [so] what is this birthright to me?' יַעֲקֹב, Ya'akov said, 'Swear to me today.' And [Esav] swore to him, and sold his birthright to יַעֲקֹב, Ya'akov.... And עֵשָׂו, Esav despised the birthright." בְּרֵאשִׁית B'reshiyt 25:30-34

Ever since they shared the womb, Ya'akov and Esav had been struggling over the birthright—but this was the day these two finally showed their true colors. Though Ya'akov's character is foreshadowed for us by his unabashed opportunism, it is Esav's behavior that is most telling. Knowing full well what he was giving up, Esav chose the fleeting moment over the future. His decision reflects something far deeper than self-absorption and near-sightedness—Esav didn't care about what really mattered... Esav *"despised the birthright."*

Like Esav, we too are always wanting what we don't have, thinking we will die if we don't get it. But worse than that, like Esav, we are willing to give up our futures because we despise and take for granted what we have already. Though there is a deceiver just waiting for the opportunity to take advantage of us, let us not give in to what we feel we need *right now*, and instead endeavor to hold on to the future—the birthright that is ours to lose.

> "יַעֲקֹב, Ya'akov came in to [Yitz'chak] his father [and Yitz'chak (who could no longer see) said]…, 'Who are *you, my son?' And* יַעֲקֹב, *Ya'akov said to* [Yitz'chak]…, 'I am עֵשָׂו, *Esav your firstborn…'* And יִצְחָק, *Yitz'chak said to* יַעֲקֹב, *Ya'akov, 'Come near, please, that I [may] feel you, my son, whether you are he, my son* עֵשָׂו, *Esav, or not.' And* יַעֲקֹב, *Ya'akov came near to… his father, and he felt him, and said, 'The voice is the voice of* יַעֲקֹב, *Ya'akov, but the hands [are the] hands of* עֵשָׂו, *Esav.' And he did not recognize him, because his hands had been [disguised to feel] hairy, as the hands of* עֵשָׂו, *Esav his brother. And he blessed him, and said, '…peoples [will] serve you, and nations [will] bow themselves to you. Be mighty over your brothers, that the sons of your mother [will] bow themselves to you. Those who curse you* will be *cursed, and those who bless you* will be *blessed.'"* בְּרֵאשִׁית
> B'reshiyt 27:18-29

The most stupefying part of this story is not that Ya'akov—in spite of being so thoroughly deceitful—still received the blessing and eventually became the father of our great nation, Yis'rael. What is *truly* astounding is that Yitz'chak actually fell for it! Our tendency is to go easy on Yitz'chak since he was old and dim in sight, but Yitz'chak made the same dumb mistake that many of us make on a daily basis: he was so caught up with his *feelings* that *he didn't listen to the voice.*

All too often, we fail to pay attention to the obvious clues—indeed, Yitz'chak knew that something was up. First, he *questioned* Ya'akov, because it was unusual and completely unexpected to receive the meal so quickly. Then, rightly doubting Ya'akov, he touched him and was taken in by what he *felt*. Finally, he smelled Ya'akov (27:27)—and since the aroma was *familiar*, he bought the entire lie. The one thing that didn't add up—the most *important* thing—was not enough to dissuade Yitz'chak from believing what he *wanted* to believe. If Yitz'chak had listened to the voice, the lie would have been immediately unraveled. But in the end, he refused to *trust* what he heard in the voice, and instead acted not on the *facts,* but on the deceptive nature of his *feelings.*

Though the voice of Ya'akov was ringing clear and true in Yitz'chak's ears, he just wouldn't listen. Like Yitz'chak, we are also quick to believe what we want, even when the voice of truth is speaking right in our face. Since what we "know" in the flesh doesn't always tell the whole story, we must learn to listen for the voice of our Master. We need to train ourselves to recognize it—and hear His voice alone—that we may always find the truth between the limitless lies of life.

❧ ❦

ADONAI, I bless You and thank You for giving me a birthright and a blessing that no one can ever take away. May I never despise what You have given me, nor be led astray by the confusion and distractions of life. Let me know You, Father, that I will never be fooled by what I *think* or *feel* is You—help me to always follow only when You are fully *known.* Speak to me, ADONAI; pronounce volumes in my ear, that I may learn how to recognize Your voice—to bless You, to touch You—and to follow You alone...

ויצא

And He Went Out
בְּרֵאשִׁית B'reshiyt (Genesis) 28:10-32:2(3)

"And [Ya'akov] dreamed, and behold, [there was] a ladder set up on the earth, and its head touched the heavens. And behold, messengers of God were going up and coming down on it. And behold, ADONAI was standing upon it, and He said, 'I am ADONAI, God of אַבְרָהָם, Av'raham your father, and God of יִצְחָק, Yitz'chak! The land on which you are lying, to you I give it, and to your descendants....' And יַעֲקֹב, Ya'akov awoke out of his sleep, and said, 'Surely ADONAI is in this place, and I [did] not know.' And he was awestruck, and said, 'How awesome is this place—this is nothing but the house of God, and this [is] a gate of the heavens.' And יַעֲקֹב, Ya'akov rose early in the morning, and took the stone which he had made his pillows, and made it a standing pillar, and poured oil upon its top, and he called the name of that place בֵּית־אֵל, Beit-el—house of God...." בְּרֵאשִׁית B'reshiyt 28:12-13, 16-19

Sometimes, when we are running from trouble, we end up in the most unusual places. In the midst of his flight from his brother, Ya'akov stumbled upon the one place on earth where he most needed to be.

So often, we're running—running away from our past, and running after something we think will be more fulfilling. But how often do we consider that where we find ourselves right now is exactly the place God wants us to be? Is ADONAI's reach so short that He cannot bring us to Himself unless *we* move *ourselves* just a little bit closer? Life at this moment may not be what *we* would like, but despite our restlessness, isn't it possible that *"ADONAI is in this place, and I [did] not know"*?

"This place" where we are now may not be what we were expecting—but God is here with us, nonetheless. We may have even been camping here for quite some time now, wondering when God will move us on. But perhaps the reason we're still here is because *here* is right where we need to be. Maybe He's been waiting for us to stop long enough to notice that He's been atop our "ladder" all along.

Sometimes when we are running, we end up in the most unusual places. Take care to mark this spot today, because you'll be back here again before you know it....

> *"And* יַעֲקֹב*, Ya'akov vowed a vow, saying, 'If God is with me, and keeps me in this way which I am going, and gives to me bread to eat, and a garment to put on—when I have returned in peace to the house of my father, then* ADONAI *will become my God, and this stone which I have made a standing pillar will [be] a house of God, and all that You will give to me, I [will] tithe [a] tenth to You.'"* בְּרֵאשִׁית *B'reshiyt 28:20-22*

Ya'akov was in awe, having found himself in the same place with God—but, like us, he didn't know when to quit while he was ahead. Despite the fact that ADONAI had revealed himself to Ya'akov in a dream, reaffirmed the covenant He had made with Av'raham and Yitz'chak, and even explicitly told Ya'akov, "*Behold, I* am *with you, and will keep you wherever you go*" (28:15), Ya'akov just couldn't believe it. Even though he was moved to set up a standing pillar in the name of God, he still wanted ADONAI to prove His faithfulness by demonstrating the truth of His Word.

"*If God is with me, and keeps me in this way which I am going, and gives to me*" this, and provides for me that, and does whatever I expect Him to do whenever I require Him to do it… "*then ADONAI will become my God.*"

For someone like Ya'akov—someone with a history of underhandedness and deceit—it's no wonder he would take a "wait and see" approach with the Lord. As disciples of Messiah, however, we would do better to take God at His Word, and behave according to our belief, rather than setting up hoops for God to jump through.

The standing pillar has been established. May the foundation of the house of God be laid in our lives without question—that the way we go will be with God.

Lord God of Av'raham, Yitz'chak *and Ya'akov*—I praise You, for Your faithfulness is everlasting. Forgive me for not seeing You in this place, and for continually second-guessing Your word. Teach me to never wander from Your ways, but to press forward according to Your word with the confidence that You are with me. ADONAI, You are my God—may my running come to an end, save only my running after You. I bless Your holy Name, for Your word is trustworthy and true, and I will follow You wholeheartedly all of my days….

וישלח

And He Sent
בְּרֵאשִׁית B'reshiyt (Genesis) 32:3(4)-36:43

"And יַעֲקֹב, Ya'akov was left alone, and [a]
man wrestled with him until the ascending of the
dawn. And [when the man] saw that he was not
able to overpower him, he struck the socket of
[Ya'akov's] thigh…. And [the man] said, 'Let me
[go] away, for the dawn has ascended.' And
[Ya'akov] said, 'I [will] not let you [go] away until
you have blessed me.' And [the man] said to him,
'What is your name?' And he said, 'יַעֲקֹב, Ya'akov.'
And [the man] said, 'Your name will no more [be]
called יַעֲקֹב, Ya'akov, but יִשְׂרָאֵל, Yis'rael, for you
have persevered with God and with men, and have
prevailed.' …And יַעֲקֹב, Ya'akov called the name
of the place פְּנוּאֵל, P'nuel, for 'I have seen God face
to face…'" בְּרֵאשִׁית B'reshiyt 32:24(25)-31(32)

What Ya'akov lacked in judgment, he made up for
in tenacity. Though taking advantage of people was
Ya'akov's strong suit, on this night he was finally unable
to get the upper hand. Not one for losing, Ya'akov
instead managed to hold out all night, ultimately forced
to settle for a draw.

But was the contest worth the cost?

Though Ya'akov successfully wrestled a blessing out of God, it nevertheless left him limping from the mat. Like Ya'akov, we often struggle with God as well, coming away from the match a little beat up. We fight with God as if we might win; we hold Him down as if we could force Him to stay. What are we thinking when we go up against God?

Too often, we contend with God for His blessing rather than simply being *content* to be with Him. Like Ya'akov, we *should* hold on and refuse to let go—but not just to get the blessing. Rather than struggling with Him for what He already wants to give us, let us hold on to Him for dear life—giving up the fight, and allowing Him to take us wherever *He* wants us to go.

> "And יַעֲקֹב, Ya'akov said to his household, and to all who were with him, 'Turn aside [from] the gods of the foreigner which are in your midst— cleanse yourselves, and change your garments. And [then] we [will] rise, and go up to בֵּית־אֵל, Beit-el, and I [will] make there an altar to God, who has answered me in the day of my distress, and is with me in the way that I have gone.' And they gave to יַעֲקֹב, Ya'akov all the gods of the foreigner that were in their hands, and the rings that were in their ears, and יַעֲקֹב, Ya'akov hid them… And [as] they journeyed, the terror of God was on the cities which were round about them, and they [did] not pursue the sons of יַעֲקֹב, Ya'akov." בְּרֵאשִׁית B'reshiyt 35:2-5

A life of running, deceit and lies… finally, it is all behind him. Ya'akov met his match in Aᴅᴏɴᴀɪ, and has at last experienced an everlasting change—He is ready to enter fully into God's blessing. Ya'akov proclaims

God the victor in the battle for his heart, confessing that *"God, who has answered me in the day of my distress... is with me in the way that I have gone."* The Lord is with Ya'akov, and no matter how much Ya'akov struggles against Him, God will never leave.

For all of us who have wrestled with God—who have fought against Him for control of our paths—it is our time to confess that God is with us... and then to *"rise, and go up."* Let us *"turn aside [from] the gods of the foreigner which are in [our] midst—cleanse [ourselves], and change [our] garments. And [then] we [will] rise, and go up to"* the House of God, and set up a testimony to His promises and blessing.

Rise, and go up—let us renounce all our idols.

Rise, and go up—let us turn wholeheartedly to God.

Rise, and go up—let us walk boldly as the *"terror of God"* goes before us, stilling all who would give pursuit.

It is time to take our stand for the One who will always stand for us—so let us *rise, and go up...*

৵৽ ৵৽

Abba, Father—my healer, and my protection—I have struggled against You, and I am in pain. Thank You, ADONAI, that I no longer have to fight—now please heal me and change my name. Help me to entrust my life to You, Lord; never leave me, but stay with me in every way that I go. I praise You for Your faithfulness, my God and my strength... teach me to rely on Your way alone. I concede, Lord—I give up! The victory is Yours! From now on, Father, instead of Your faithful wounds, may I know the overflowing joy of Your blessing...

Vayeshev

וישב

And He Dwelled
בְּרֵאשִׁית B'reshiyt (Genesis) 37:1-40:23

*"And [Yosef] said, 'Behold, I have dreamed a
dream again... the sun and the moon, and eleven
stars were bowing themselves to me.' And he
recounted [it] to his father, and to his brothers; and
his father pushed against him, and said to him,
'What is this dream which you have dreamt? Do
we certainly come—I, and your mother, and your
brothers—to bow ourselves to you, to the earth?'
And his brothers were zealous against him...."*
בְּרֵאשִׁית *B'reshiyt 37:9-11*

Young men rarely have good judgment, even when
they have the mind of God. At seventeen, Yosef was no
exception. Had Yosef dreamed such dreams as a man of
some years, he might have shown more discretion in
recounting them to his family. As such, his brothers
may have had considerably less reason to hate him, and
he might have arrived at his destiny by a different path.

Though he was neither lying nor exaggerating in the
telling of his dreams, Yosef would have done well to
temper his candid foreknowledge with humility. Like
Yosef, we must never be afraid to speak the truth at all
times. And yet, we need to be careful to not run ahead

of God, lifting ourselves up in the process—especially when we think we know what's coming.

> *"And ADONAI was with יוֹסֵף, Yosef, and he became a prosperous man. And he was in the house of his [Egyptian] master…. [who] saw that ADONAI was with [Yosef]. And all that he was doing, ADONAI was causing to prosper in his hand…."* בְּרֵאשִׁית *B'reshiyt 39:2-3*

From the angry hands of his brothers to indentured servitude in Mitz'rayim, Yosef was nonetheless on the path toward his destiny. At home with Yis'rael, Yosef had clearly been the favorite among the sons. Now, owned by Mitz'rayim, he was receiving the favor of the Lord. Despite his troubled circumstances, *"all that he was doing, ADONAI was causing to prosper in his hand… and he became a prosperous man… and his master saw that ADONAI was with [him]."*

Like Yosef, we too may display evidence that ADONAI is with us—but also like Yosef, ADONAI's favor does not guarantee our release from unfavorable circumstances. Indeed, things may get much, much worse before they show signs of getting any better—yet this does not diminish ADONAI's approval of how we are living for Him. May we take solace in the favor that the Lord is showing us today, even if it means waiting for our vindication and destiny just a little while longer.

> *"And [there in the prison,] ADONAI was with יוֹסֵף, Yosef and stretched out kindness to him…. [Some time later, Pharaoh put] the chief butler, and… the chief baker… in prison…. One night, they each dreamed a dream… [and] in the*

morning, [Yosef] saw them, and behold, they were
fretful…. And they said to [Yosef], 'A dream we
have dreamed, but there is no [one to] interpret…'
And יוֹסֵף, *Yosef said… 'Are not interpretations*
[according] to God? Please, tell it to me.'"
בְּרֵאשִׁית *B'reshiyt 39:21, 40:2-3, 5-8*

Seasoned by the trials of life, Yosef shed all signs of
youthful arrogance and pride. In the midst of humbling
circumstances, he found humility—even as ADONAI
faithfully and repeatedly raised him up. When it came
time once again to exercise his unique gift, it seems he
had learned his lesson. Rather than being quick to exalt
himself, he humbly acknowledged the truth: *"Are not*
interpretations [according] to God?"

Any gift we may have, any prosperity or success…
the mature man gives all the glory to God. May we
therefore learn Yosef's lesson well: humility will do its
full work in us—one way or another. Since we all may
eventually find ourselves trapped in the bottom of that
pit, we need to see the Lord alone as our *only* hope for
getting out. Anything else… and we're just *dreaming…*

෨ ෪

ADONAI, I praise Your Name, for You lead me day
by day according to Your excellent ways. Though You
humble me, Lord, You never leave me—thank You for
lifting up my head, showing me favor and approval even
in the most discouraging circumstances. I bless You, O
God, for You reveal the end from the beginning—only
let me not run ahead of You, thinking I know more than
I actually do. Teach me humility and patience, ADONAI,
as I wait for You to make all my dreams come true….

מִקֵץ

At the End
בְּרֵאשִׁית B'reshiyt (Genesis) 41:1-44:17

*"And פַּרְעֹה, Par'oh said to יוֹסֵף, Yosef, 'A
dream I have dreamed, and there is no interpreter
of it, and I—I have heard concerning you, that
you [can] understand a dream and interpret it.'
And יוֹסֵף, Yosef answered פַּרְעֹה, Par'oh, saying,
'Without me, God will answer פַּרְעֹה, Par'oh with
peace.'" בְּרֵאשִׁית B'reshiyt 41:15-16*

After being restored to Par'oh's service, Yosef's
cellmate forgot all about him—so for another two years,
Yosef remained in prison, awaiting his deliverance. But
even though he failed to receive immediate recognition
for interpreting the butler's dream, Yosef's reputation
went before him at the moment that it mattered most.

And yet, he gave God all the credit for what he was
about to do.

When Yosef was presented with what Par'oh had
"heard concerning [him]," instead of accepting the
acclaim, Yosef denied himself by saying, *"without me."*
Would we be so quick to discard our own good name
and instead promote the reputation of God?

"And יוֹסֵף, Yosef said to פַּרְעֹה, Par'oh, 'The dreams of פַּרְעֹה, Par'oh are one [and the same]: that which God will do He has revealed to פַּרְעֹה, Par'oh.... And because of the repeating of the dream to פַּרְעֹה, Par'oh twice, surely the word has been fixed by God, and God is hastening to do it.'" בְּרֵאשִׁית *B'reshiyt 41:25,32*

Perhaps if we got out of God's way long and often enough, His reputation in our minds would be restored. Too often, however, we wonder what God is up to—speculating about what He is doing while trying to plan our next move. Instead, we ought to rely on His unshakable character, confident that He reveals everything we need to know.

The word of ADONAI *"has been fixed by God,"* so we should find peace by trusting what He says to us. His reputation is excellent, His word is always true, and He shows us His plans at the perfect time—if only we would open our eyes to see them. Let us, then, stop second-guessing God, and instead get on board and out of His way. Let us trust that everything He has promised, in *His* time, *"God is hastening to do it."*

"And the word was good in the eyes of פַּרְעֹה, Par'oh, [and he] said to his servants, 'Can we find a man like this in whom is רוּחַ אֱלֹהִים, Ruach 'Elohiym?' And פַּרְעֹה, Par'oh said to יוֹסֵף, Yosef, 'Since God's causing you to know all this, there is none [as] discerning and wise as you. You—you are [now] over my house, and at your mouth will all my people kiss....'" בְּרֵאשִׁית *B'reshiyt 41:37-40*

God used Yosef because he was willing to step aside and let the Ruach in him be seen. The son of Yis'rael

was not unique in Mitz'rayim just because he was a
Hebrew, or because he alone knew the God of his father.
Yosef was an exceptional man because he learned that
the Spirit of God makes us who we are. The more we
remove the attention from ourselves and allow God to
make *Himself* known in us, the more men will honor
and praise *our* name... to the honor and praise of God.

Yosef's discernment and wisdom were his because
of *"God's causing [him] to know all this."* Like Yosef, we
may also own such excellent qualities that define us as
followers of God—but if we truly want to have a name
as good as the Lord's, we would do well to make
ourselves of no repute. So let us not be elevated and
admired because we deserve the applause. Rather, let us
allow God in us to shine—*despite* ourselves—for He is
the One who has made us exactly as we are supposed to
be.

అ ఆ

Lord God, may You alone be seen in me, that I may
never be seen at all. I praise You, ADONAI—let *Your*
reputation precede me, so that all glory offered to me
may be given to Your Name. Teach me, Father, to trust
in Your unchanging word and to rely not on my own
understanding. Remind me of Your promises, and grant
me the patience to wait until they come to pass. I bless
You, God of my fathers—I am getting on board and out
of Your way. Thank You, O Lord, for revealing Your
word to this servant, and for doing all Your great works
without me...

And He Came Near
בְּרֵאשִׁית B'reshiyt (Genesis) 44:18-47:27

"And יוֹסֵף, Yosef said to his brothers, 'Come near to me, please,' and they came near; and he said, 'I am יוֹסֵף, Yosef, your brother, whom you sold into מִצְרַיִם, Mitz'rayim. And now, [do] not be grieved, nor let it be angering in your eyes that you sold me here, for God has sent me before you to preserve life. For these two years the famine has been in the heart of the land, and [there] will be five years yet before there is either plowing or harvest. Therefore God sent me before you, to place a remnant of you in the land, and to give life to you by a great escape. And now you—you have not sent me here, but God...."' בְּרֵאשִׁית B'reshiyt 45:4-7

In total shock and terror, the sons of Yis'rael finally knew the truth: their brother Yosef was not only alive—he was their master…

… and savior of all Yis'rael.

Though the end had been revealed from the beginning, no one could have guessed the path they would take to get there. That the brothers of Yosef would leave him for dead only to later find their fate in his hands was unimaginable. But Yosef comforted and assured his brothers, *"You have not sent me here, but God...."*

The idea that ADONAI would use the suffering of one man to redeem and preserve life for all is beyond our comprehension. Allowing an innocent person to endure pain for even a moment screams of injustice—the sadistic cruelty of a wrathful God. And yet, this is exactly what the Lord did through Yosef, whose trials and affliction we not merely permitted by God, but orchestrated by Him *"to preserve life... and to give life... by a great escape."*

Just as Yosef humbly accepted his role in the salvation of his people, so did our brother, Yeshua, who died for the sins of the world. He, too, suffered false accusation and imprisonment; He, too, endured the hatred of His brothers. And like Yosef, the Messiah Yeshua is now in a position of power and authority *"to preserve life... and to give life... by a great escape."*

One day, in total shock and terror, the sons of Yis'rael will finally know the truth: our brother Yeshua is not only alive—He is our Master... and savior of all Yis'rael...

... indeed, the whole world.

"And God spoke to יִשְׂרָאֵל, Yis'rael in visions of the night, and said, 'יַעֲקֹב, יַעֲקֹב, Ya'akov, Ya'akov,' and he said, 'Here I am.' And He said, 'אָנֹכִי הָאֵל, anochiy HaEl (I am God), God of your father—be not afraid of going down to מִצְרַיִם, Mitz'rayim, for [it is] for a great nation [that] I set you there. I— I go down with you to מִצְרַיִם, Mitz'rayim, and I— I also certainly [will] bring you up. And יוֹסֵף, Yosef

will put his hand on [you and close] your eyes.'"
בְּרֵאשִׁית *B'reshiyt 46:2-4*

What the children of Yis'rael would find in
Mitz'rayim, Ya'akov did not know. Would they be the
ones God spoke to Av'ram about—the ones who would
be oppressed and enslaved for generations to come? All
Ya'akov knew was that his long-lost son Yosef was found
in that foreign land, and that HaEl told him to have no
fear—that it was *"for a great nation [that] I set you there."*

We may not always know in advance how God is
going to get us to where He wants us to be. We may
sometimes even see the place He's taking us and be
afraid of where we're inevitably headed. But as surely as
He is going down with us to the place we are afraid to
go, we can be confident that He will remember His
promises to us and deliver us from death once again.

"And [He]—[He] also certainly [will] bring you up."

୬ ୭

Lord God of Av'raham and Ya'akov, Redeemer of
Yis'rael, I praise Your great Name. Who is like You,
ADONAI, who plans the end from the beginning, and
uses the anguish and pain of One to accomplish the
salvation of all? I bless You, Father, for sending Your
humble servant, Yeshua, to preserve and give life by a
great escape. Thank You, Lord, for using me as You see
fit—may my use in Your kingdom be as selfless and
honorable as that of Your Son. Teach me, ADONAI, to
be satisfied with the knowledge that You alone can quiet
all fears—and that even in the shadow of suffering,
O God, You firmly hold my salvation in Your hands...

ויחי

And He Lived
בְּרֵאשִׁית B'reshiyt (Genesis) 47:28-50:26

*"יְהוּדָה, Y'hudah! You—your brothers [will]
praise you! Your hand will be on the neck of your
enemies; [the] sons of your father [will] bow
themselves to you. יְהוּדָה, Y'hudah is a lion's
young—for prey, my son, you have gone up. He is
bent [down], he is crouched like a lion; and as a
lioness, who causes him to arise? The scepter [will]
turn not aside from יְהוּדָה, Y'hudah, nor the ruling
staff from between his feet, until שִׁילֹה, Shiyloh
comes, and his will be the obedience of [the]
peoples." בְּרֵאשִׁית B'reshiyt 49:8-10*

Before breathing his last, Ya'akov spoke blessings
over his sons, pronouncing one of the greatest over
infamous Y'hudah. Second only to that of Yosef, the
word to Y'hudah speaks of his resolve and strength, his
passion and readiness—his headship. Ya'akov declared
that Y'hudah and his descendants would lead the sons
of Yis'rael—that *"the scepter [will] not turn aside"* from
him. But the ruling staff does not belong to Y'hudah—
he is merely its caretaker *"until Shiyloh comes."*

As Y'hudah would be master of Yis'rael, Shiyloh—
the One to whom authority belongs—will be the Master

of all... *"the obedience of [the] peoples"* will be His. In the same way that Y'hudah would be praised among Yis'rael, the Master, too—who is *of* Y'hudah—will receive praise. May we submit to the rulership of Shiyloh—the Messiah Yeshua—even as we eagerly await His arrival. Let us look forward to the Day when He will forever take up the scepter that Y'hudah is keeping in his care.

> *"And the brothers of* יוֹסֵף, *Yosef saw that their father was dead, and said, 'What if* יוֹסֵף, *Yosef hates us and will certainly return to us all the evil which we did to him.' And they gave a charge to* יוֹסֵף, *Yosef, saying, 'Your father commanded before his death, saying, "...Please, please, forgive the transgression of your brothers, and their sin, for they have done you evil. And now, please, forgive the transgression of the servants of the God of your father."' And* יוֹסֵף, *Yosef wept.... And his brothers also went and fell before him, and said, 'Behold, we* are *to you for servants.' And* יוֹסֵף, *Yosef said to them, 'Fear not, for* am *I in the place of God? As for you, you devised against me evil—God devised it for good, in order to do as at* this *day, to keep alive a numerous people. And now, fear not: I nourish you and your children.' And he comforted them, and spoke to their heart."* בְּרֵאשִׁית *B'reshiyt 50:15-21*

What seemed to be a dead issue was apparently alive and well in the hearts of Yosef's brothers. For years they lived in Mitz'rayim side-by-side with Yosef, all the while hiding their trepidation over the day of their father's passing—they believed their brother would take his revenge on them once Ya'akov was no longer alive.

As Yosef's brothers pled with him for their lives, he was brought to tears by the realization that even after all this time, they still did not understand. *"As for you, you devised against me evil—God devised it for good,"* and through Yosef's suffering, ADONAI brought life to His people… *"he comforted them, and spoke to their heart."* How could they live in the presence of their deliverer and still be afraid he would hold their sins against them?

Like the brothers of Yosef, we too are often fearful of approaching our Deliverer. Even though all has been forgotten, we think our past sins are too grievous for forgiveness—that the Lord will still count them against us and take His revenge. So we beg and plead for our lives, hoping beyond hope that He will spare us. We fall before Him trembling in desperate servitude, praying for pity and the staying of His wrath.

But like Yosef, the Messiah Yeshua—our Deliverer—does not *"hate us"* or desire to *"return to us all the evil"* which we have done. On the contrary, He has forgiven our transgression and sin, and He weeps when we fear Him, desiring only to comfort us and speak to our hearts. It is for life that He delivered us, not to enslave us to fear of death. May we—and all the sons of Yis'rael—come into the presence of our Deliverer, no longer afraid that He will hold our sins against us.

გ∕ დ

Deliverer and Ruler of Yis'rael, King Messiah, You are worthy of all praise! I eagerly await the season of Your coming when You reign with Y'hudah's scepter—yet today I accept the comforting of Your Spirit, and in Your presence receive complete forgiveness of my sins. Shiyloh, You are ruler of my life, of Yis'rael, and of all the peoples. I bless You, my King, for You take away all fear, nourishing me with Your word as You speak life to my heart…

שמות

Sh'mot · Exodus

שמות

Names
שְׁמוֹת Sh'mot (Exodus) 1:1-6:1

> *"And ADONAI said, 'I have certainly seen the
> affliction of My people... in מִצְרַיִם, Mitz'rayim.
> And their cry—because of their oppressors—I
> have heard, for I have known their pains. And I go
> down to deliver them out of the hand of the מִצְרַיִם,
> Mitz'rayim, and to cause them to go up out of the
> land, to a land good and broad, to a land flowing
> with milk and honey....'" שְׁמוֹת Sh'mot 3:7-8*

Deliverance begins with a cry for help. In their
slavery, Yis'rael toiled for years on end, serving the will
of oppressive Mitz'rayim. But even though ADONAI had
"certainly seen the affliction of [His] people," it wasn't
until their cries went up to Him that He called forth His
Deliverer.

Sometimes we feel that the Lord is not responding
quickly enough to our needs, and we wonder what is
taking Him so long. Could it be that we have not truly
come to the end of ourselves, and cried out to Him as
the only source of our deliverance? Surely, ADONAI will
come down and *"cause [us] to go up out of the land"* of
our affliction—but maybe He is waiting to *"go down to
deliver"* us until we realize just how much we need Him.

> "And מֹשֶׁה, Moshe said to Aᴅᴏɴᴀɪ, '…I am
> not a man of words, either yesterday, or before, or
> since Your speaking to Your servant—for I am
> slow of mouth and slow of tongue.' And Aᴅᴏɴᴀɪ
> said to him, 'Who appointed a mouth for man?
> Or who appointed the dumb, or deaf, or seeing, or
> blind? Is it not I, Aᴅᴏɴᴀɪ? And now, go, and I—I
> am with your mouth, and will direct you [in] that
> which you speak.' And [Moshe] said, '…send
> [another], please—by [someone else's] hand will
> You send [Your message].'" שְׁמוֹת Sh'mot 4:10-13

Perhaps we don't want to admit how much we need
God for fear that it will obligate us to His service. Moshe,
for instance, offered every objection and excuse he could
imagine in order to skirt the responsibility being placed
on him by the Lord. Aᴅᴏɴᴀɪ's response was pointed:
you are who I made you to be—now stop your whining,
and do as I say.

Aᴅᴏɴᴀɪ has appointed a specific and unique task for
each of us to perform. Who are we to talk back to the
Creator, requesting that He give our job to someone
else? He knows how He made us, and He knows what
He's doing. Let us, therefore, stop making excuses and
start making headway in our lives for Messiah… because
"dumb, or deaf, or seeing, or blind," He is sending us
with a message—and He has equipped us to go.

> "And מֹשֶׁה, Moshe turned back to Aᴅᴏɴᴀɪ,
> and said, 'Master, why have You done evil to this
> people? Why is this? You have sent me! And since
> I have come to פַּרְעֹה, Par'oh, to speak in Your
> Name, he has done evil to this people, and You
> have not delivered Your people at all.' And
> Aᴅᴏɴᴀɪ said to מֹשֶׁה, Moshe, 'Now will you see
> that which I do….'" שְׁמוֹת Sh'mot 5:22-6:1

Considering Moshe's failed attempts to avoid his destiny, it's no wonder that he was a little bit upset when things didn't go as planned. After all, it was ADONAI who had sent him back to Mitz'rayim—and it was ADONAI's instructions he was following to the letter—surely, it was ADONAI who had *"done evil to this people"* by clearly *"not deliver[ing His] people at all."* In fact, the people of Yis'rael were worse off now than before Moshe opened his big mouth. *"Why* is *this?"*

When the Lord sends us to do His will, the result of our going is irrelevant. We will be used as He sees fit, and His purposes will be accomplished regardless of the outcome we expect or experience. ADONAI is going before us to do a great and mighty work that will glorify His Name. Let us be satisfied to do our part in bringing about the deliverance of ADONAI, and then watch and wait on the Lord—for *"now will you see that which I do…"*

કર્જી ન્હ્છ

ADONAI, I bless Your Name—take the selfishness and self-doubt away, and throw it in the fire. I praise You, Abba, for You never leave me unequipped for the life I am facing, but You hear and answer my every heart-cry—You come down just to bring me out. You are worthy of all glory and honor, ADONAI, and I need You far more than I realize. Teach me to rely upon You for all of my days, knowing that Your plans will never fail—even when they include me….

Vaera

וָאֵרָא

And I Appeared
שְׁמוֹת Sh'mot (Exodus) 6:2-9:35

"And מֹשֶׁה, Moshe said to פַּרְעֹה, Par'oh, 'Glorify yourself over me; [you may choose] when I will pray for you and for your servants and for your people, to cut off the frogs from you and from your houses....' And [Par'oh] said, 'Tomorrow.' And [Moshe] replied, 'According to your word it will be, *so that you [will] know that there is none like* ADONAI *our God....'"* שְׁמוֹת *Sh'mot 8:9(5)-10(6)*

He is not some unknowable God—ambiguous, faceless, and hard to find. ADONAI is not only knowable, but He actually wants to be known. Why?—so that we can see *"that there is none like* ADONAI *our God."* For this reason, He may choose to offer us a glimpse into His greatness, allowing *us* to affect *His* plans. He does this so we will know that He is alive, and that He hears the words and desires of all.

Daily, ADONAI our God gives us the opportunity to know Him more. When He lets us fill in the blanks— to write our own story, as it were—it is a sobering reminder of His continual presence. May we never take for granted the fact that He is listening, but instead speak a word worth saying... because when He responds, He is sure to be fully known: the One and Only God.

> *"For if you do not let My people go... I will send against you... a swarm [of insects].... But I will set apart in that day the land of* גֹּשֶׁן, *Goshen, in which My people are staying, that the swarm will not [be] there, so that you [will] know that I am ADONAI in the midst of the land, and I will make a distinction between My people and your people...."* שְׁמוֹת *Sh'mot 8:21(17)a, 22-23(18-19)*

ADONAI treats His people differently than He treats everyone else. Is it because He loves us more? Are we simply better than everyone else? No, He *"make[s] a distinction between [His] people"* and the rest of the nations *"so that you [will] know that I am ADONAI."* He singles us out not because we're so special, but so that *His* greatness will be acknowledged. He distinguishes those who belong to Him for the sake of His glory alone.

Since ADONAI sets us apart for the whole world to see, one question remains: what are we supposed to do with all this attention? Perhaps we are not overrun with frogs and flies—but what good is such chosenness if we are caught in a swarm of selfishness and sin? All eyes are watching the distinguished people of God—should we not make certain that our behavior is commensurate with our calling? Let us not desecrate the platform with which we have been entrusted, but instead act according to the distinction of knowing ADONAI, our God.

> *"...at this time I will send all My plagues to your heart [Par'oh]... so that you [will] know that there is none like Me in all the earth. For at any time I [could] have put forth My hand and...*

*struck you and your people with [a] plague and you
[would] have been wiped from the earth. And yet,
for this [purpose] I have caused you to stand, so as
to show you My power, and for the sake of declaring
My Name in all the earth...."* שְׁמוֹת *Sh'mot 9:14-16*

ADONAI makes Himself known by allowing us to be
part of His plans. He makes Himself known by setting
His people apart, giving us a platform from which to
shine. But He also makes Himself known by raising up
and setting apart the wicked—not so they may triumph,
but so that He may make an example of them. ADONAI
causes His enemies to stand *"so as to show... [His] power,
and for the sake of declaring [His] Name in all the earth."*

For all time, Mitz'rayim serves as an example for
those who would presume to oppose the will of God. Let
us receive the warning in earnest and consider how *we*
might fare should our hearts be hardened to the God of
Yis'rael. For the sons of men, ADONAI has always wanted
just one thing: for us to know Him. May we know Him,
then, not by His wrath, but by the patience and mercy
He continually displays... even as we constantly seem to
forget that He alone is God.

ও ⚘

That You may be known, ADONAI, display Your
glory and greatness! I praise You, Lord, for there truly
is none like You in all the earth. Thank You, Father, for
holding back Your hand, even though I am constantly
taking You for granted. Show me Your ways, ADONAI,
that I may know You more, never forgetting that You
are God. I bless You, Mighty One of Yis'rael, who sets
apart both the wicked and the righteous. I give glory to
Your great Name alone, ADONAI—the One True and
Holy God!

Bo

ב

בא

Go
שְׁמוֹת Sh'mot (Exodus) 10:1-13:16

*"And the servants of פַּרְעֹה, Par'oh said to him,
'How long will this* man *be a snare to us? Send the
men away, so they [will] serve* ADONAI *their God.
[Do] you not yet know that מִצְרַיִם, Mitz'rayim is
destroyed?'"* שְׁמוֹת *Sh'mot 10:7*

After seven increasingly devastating plagues upon
Mitz'rayim, it was obvious to everyone how the whole
standoff was going to end—obvious to everyone, that is,
except Par'oh... he just didn't get it. As Par'oh continually
failed to humble himself before God, ADONAI's display of
power escalated—and yet, Par'oh remained unconvinced
to let the people of Yis'rael go. He couldn't see the future
that was so plainly set before him.

Like Par'oh, we too tend to stare straight into the
face of destiny, while refusing to see what is right there
in plain sight. When we stand rigidly opposed to the
will and plans of God, we can be assured of how
everything will end. Instead, we need to respond to
God with all humility, and then leave the decision of
our fate up to Him. Ultimately, the Lord is going to
win the conflict over our lives... let's face it—we can
see it coming.

"And ADONAI strengthened [the resolve of] the heart of פַּרְעֹה, Par'oh, and he was not willing to let [Yis'rael] go. And פַּרְעֹה, Par'oh said to [Moshe], 'Go from me, [and] guard yourself—see my face no more—for in the day you see my face [again,] you will die.' And מֹשֶׁה, Moshe said, 'Rightly have you spoken—I will see your face no more.'"
שְׁמוֹת *Sh'mot 10:27-29*

The fate of Mitz'rayim was sealed when, time after time, Par'oh strengthened his resolve against ADONAI. It ought to strike *us* with fear and dread, however, to know that ADONAI *Himself* played an active role in the hardening of Par'oh's heart. Once Par'oh had fully and repeatedly set his mind on denying the sovereign power of God, the Lord made his end an inevitability... the wrath against Par'oh and Mitz'rayim would be poured out in full.

How hard, then, do our hearts have to be before ADONAI *Himself* strengthens our resolve against Him? Surely we should learn the lesson of Par'oh, and do everything in our power to avoid finding out for ourselves! Let us not allow pride to prophesy our own demise, but instead resolve to heed the word of the God of Yis'rael—standing *with*, rather than against Him. Indeed, as much as our hearts can be hardened by God, how much more can He soften them as well?

"And I will pass over through the land of מִצְרַיִם, Mitz'rayim during this night, and will strike every first-born in the land of מִצְרַיִם, Mitz'rayim, from man even to beast, and on all the gods of מִצְרַיִם, Mitz'rayim I [will] execute judgment. I am ADONAI." שְׁמוֹת *Sh'mot 12:12*

The height of ADONAI's wrath upon Mitz'rayim came that fateful night when ADONAI passed over and spared the homes of Yis'rael. ADONAI demonstrated in very certain terms that He was making a distinction between Mitz'rayim and Yis'rael—a demonstration that left no room for interpretation. And yet it was not merely upon Mitz'rayim that ADONAI showed His power, but *"on all the gods of Mitz'rayim [did He] execute judgment."* His wrath was poured out on both the followers and the followed.

The ultimate distinction between those who are with God and those who stand against Him is determined by whom we choose to serve. When ADONAI *"pass[es] over through the land,"* will He find us still clinging to the gods and idols of our lives that have already been condemned for destruction? Let us turn our backs on those *"gods"* once and for all, and instead turn to the living God of Yis'rael who will deliver us. As we are *"pass[ed] over,"* may we be identified only by the blood of the Lamb that has been faithfully applied to the doorposts of our hearts... that we may receive the salvation of the Lord...

ॐ ᴥ

ADONAI, Holy One, full of justice and mercy—I choose You, my God and my King! Completely destroy my stubbornness and pride, that my resolve to serve Your great Name may be strengthened. I bless You, ADONAI, God of power and righteousness—for You alone are worthy of all honor and praise. Execute Your judgment, O Lord, on the gods of my life, that Your word alone I may heed and obey. Thank You, Father, for the salvation of Your Son, in whom ultimate distinction and glory abounds. Soften my heart, and have mercy, O God, that I may always and forever see Your face...

B'shalach

בשלח

When He Let Go
שְׁמוֹת Sh'mot (Exodus) 13:17-17:16

*"And they said to מֹשֶׁה, Moshe, '[Is it] because
there are no graves in מִצְרַיִם, Mitz'rayim you have
taken us away to die in the wilderness? What is this
you have done to us—to bring us out from מִצְרַיִם,
Mitz'rayim? Is not this the word which we spoke to
you in מִצְרַיִם, Mitz'rayim, saying, "Leave us [alone]
that we [may] serve the מִצְרַיִם, Mitz'rayim; for [it
is] better for us to serve the מִצְרַיִם, Mitz'rayim than
to die in the wilderness!"'" שְׁמוֹת Sh'mot 14:11-12*

If you had realized in advance the high cost of
following Yeshua—that is, death to self—would you
still have signed on with Him? Just as many of us aren't
so sure we want to deny ourselves for Messiah's sake, so
did the sons of Yis'rael experience "buyer's remorse" for
their newfound freedom... they feared it would lead to
their certain demise. In the same way that Yis'rael was
strangled by her fear, so do we often wonder if the
challenge of being Messiah's is really worth it—the
challenge of losing ourselves daily to follow Him.

Threatened by the hostile enemy seeking to recapture
and overtake them, the sons of Yis'rael cried out, *"[It is]
better for us to serve the Mitz'rayim than to die in the*

wilderness!" As disciples of Yeshua, may we never fall
for the lie that it is better to live enslaved to sin than to
die free in Messiah. No matter the trials or difficulties
we face for being devoted to God, death to self is *always*
better than life to sin. Let us no longer be like Yis'rael—
temporarily blind to our salvation—but open our eyes
to the truth that dying to self yields only life… abundant
life in Messiah.

> *"And* מֹשֶׁה, *Moshe said to the people, 'Fear not,
> still yourselves, and see the salvation of* ADONAI,
> *which He does for you today. For, as you have
> seen the* מִצְרַיִם, *Mitz'rayim today, never any more
> [will you] see them again—to the age.* ADONAI
> *will fight for you. And you—[just] keep silent.'"*
> שְׁמוֹת *Sh'mot 14:13-14*

Like the slighted Mitz'rayim, sin pursues us
relentlessly. It doesn't like the fact that it lost us to God,
and—like Par'oh—when it realizes what it's done, it
renews its resolve to get us back. We, however, are sin's
willing victims when we actually *believe* that it can still
overtake us. What many of us fail to realize is that for
those who are Messiah's, the only way sin can own us
again is if we go back to it of our own accord.

On the shore of the sea, Moshe stood and declared,
*"For, as you have seen the Mitz'rayim today, never any
more [will you] see them again…."* Once salvation
comes, our deliverance is complete—we never have to
fear or go back to Mitz'rayim again. We are free once
and for all; all ties of bondage and slavery are cut. Let
us then *"still [ourselves], and see the salvation of*
ADONAI," remembering the *reality* that *"*ADONAI *will
fight for [us]"* and protect us forever from sin. *"Fear
not… you—[just] keep silent."*

> *"And* מֹשֶׁה, *Moshe stretched out his hand towards the sea, and* ADONAI *caused the sea to go on by a strong east wind all the night, and made the sea become dry ground, and the waters were cleaved. And the sons of* יִשְׂרָאֵל, *Yis'rael went into the midst of the sea on dry land, and the waters were to them a wall, on their right and on their left."* שְׁמוֹת *Sh'mot 14:21-22*

What would become a coffin for the soldiers of Mitz'rayim was the path to salvation for Yis'rael. Backed up to the sea with the Mitz'riy horde fast approaching, Yis'rael had lost all hope of escape. Death, it seemed, was the best they could expect—all roads to deliverance were apparently washed out. But then, out of nowhere, a passageway unseen was opened before them—and the sons of Yis'rael hurried on to their freedom.

When we are trapped on all sides, and it seems like there is no way out, let us have faith as we remember the walls sent to save Yis'rael. On our behalf, ADONAI will hold back even the depth of the seas—we will walk through on dry ground; then He will drown the enemy that pursues us. Look today at the impassible roads of your life, because seemingly out of nowhere, a new way is being laid for you. The Lord is raising the mighty walls of salvation that will line your way to freedom!

❧ ❧

"Who is like You among the gods, O ADONAI? *Who is like You—great in holiness… awesome in praises… doing wonders?"* Show me, O God, the path I have missed by being fearful and willfully returning to my old ways. I give You all blessing and honor, Lord, for You still all fears—Forgiver of sin, I receive Your salvation. Mighty God, I praise You; I stand still in Your presence. Thank You for loving me, ADONAI—Redeemer, Savior, *friend…*

יתרו

Jethro
שְׁמוֹת Sh'mot (Exodus) 18:1-20:26(23)

*"And יִתְרוֹ, Yit'ro said, 'Blessed is ADONAI…
who has delivered this people from under the hand
of the מִצְרַיִם, Mitz'rayim. Now I know that ADONAI
is greater than all the gods, for in the matter they
acted arrogantly—[but] He is above them!'"*
שְׁמוֹת *Sh'mot 18:10-11*

Who knows what Yit'ro was thinking when Moshe,
his son-in-law, asked to go back to Mitz'rayim. But
when Moshe returned with the news of ADONAI's glory,
Yit'ro's response was clear: *"Now I know that ADONAI is
greater than all the gods."* It was for this very reaction
that ADONAI sent Yis'rael to dwell in Mitz'rayim; it was
why the sons of Yis'rael were enslaved to Par'oh, and
why Mitz'rayim and her gods were trounced by the
hand of ADONAI—so that all the families of the earth
would *"know that ADONAI is greater than all the gods…
He is above them!"*

Let us always remember that in our victories as well
as our trials, ADONAI has a purpose and a plan—that all
will know His Name, and His Name alone will be
glorified. May we never forget that if our suffering will
produce glory for God, it is to our honor to endure such

hardship. For the sake of the nations, then, may we also be delivered from our bondage so that all will know the greatness of ADONAI—that compared to the gods of this world, our God alone is above them all.

> *"And God spoke all these words, saying, 'I am ADONAI your God, who has brought you out of the land of* מִצְרַיִם, *Mitz'rayim—out of a house of bondage. You [must] have no other gods before My [face].'"* שְׁמוֹת *Sh'mot 20:1-3*

Since ADONAI displayed His wondrous glory before us by bringing us *"out of a house of bondage,"* surely He deserves our gratefulness and thanks… but our sole allegiance? Why should ADONAI be the only recipient of our love, dedication and devotion? Isn't it somewhat arrogant to do something nice for someone—like calling them out from all the nations of the earth and freeing them from centuries of oppression and slavery— only to insist that we owe Him our exclusive loyalty and commitment?

When we serve the other "gods" of our lives—our wants, our flesh, our selves—we are parading *our* arrogance and pride in the face of God. We may think we are being discreet in how we dishonor and degrade ourselves, but when we serve other gods, we are literally *loving* them in His face—we are rubbing His nose in our adulterous rebellion.

ADONAI insists on our sole allegiance for the simple reason that He deserves it. Everything He is and all that He has done warrants our sincere and absolute devotion. Let us give God not merely the thanks, but all that is due His Name. He *alone* has delivered us from the bondage of sin—let us *"have no other gods before [His face.]"*

*"And [all the people] said to מֹשֶׁה, Moshe,
'You speak with us, and we [will] hear, but let
not God speak with us, lest we die.' And מֹשֶׁה,
Moshe said to the people, 'Fear not, for God has
come to test you, and so that His fear may be
before your faces—that you [will] sin not.'"*
שְׁמוֹת *Sh'mot 20:19-20(16-17)*

We are slow to pledge our allegiance to ADONAI
because we fear the cost of such devotion—if we allow
God to speak with us, we might actually have to *do* what
He says. And so we do not wish to hear Him, *"lest we
die,"* because to obey His word is to die to ourselves...
to give up our wants, desires and self-will, and walk in
the ways of ADONAI alone.

If ADONAI did not love us, He would leave us to our
own devices—to be consumed by our wanton, worldly
ways. But rather than remain silent, He instead comes
"to test you, and so that His fear may be before your faces."
Therefore, let us stand at the foot of the mountain in
reverent fear—not in terror of death, but humbled by
His presence. As ADONAI tests us for our obedience, may
we in turn heed His word and revere His greatness...
"that [we will] sin not."

&ン &ぅ

ADONAI, Maker of everything, You alone are greater
than all the gods! I praise You, Abba, for You deserve
blessing, honor and devotion from me all the days of my
life. Thank You for not remembering my sin and all my
adulterous ways, but instead restoring my soul to You so
that You may receive all my praise. Make Your Name
great in my life, ADONAI, that blessings to You will
abound. May I die daily for Your sake and Your glory,
and pass the test of Your incomparable holiness...

Judgments
שְׁמוֹת Sh'mot (Exodus) 21:1-24:18

*"Behold, I am sending a messenger before you
to keep you on the way, and to bring you in to the
place which I have prepared. Be watchful because
of his presence, and listen to his voice. [Do] not
rebel against him, for he [will] not bear with your
transgression—for My Name is in him..."*
שְׁמוֹת *Sh'mot 23:20-21*

As believers in Yeshua, we often make light of our
commitment to God—we are quick to receive the
blessings that He promises, but are slow to do what He
requires of us in return. We are not asked to obey
simply because He deserves our attention and obedience.
On the contrary, ADONAI expects us to do as He instructs
so that we can safely reach our destiny and fulfill our
purposes on the earth.

This is why ADONAI sent His messenger before
Yis'rael—*"to keep [them] on the way, and to bring [them]
in to the place which [He had] prepared."* In order to
enter the Promised Land, Yis'rael had to *"be watchful...
and listen"*—and, perhaps most importantly, *"not rebel."*
Obedience is more than just hearing God's word—it
means listening to that voice above our own. May we

cast aside our rebellious tendencies and instead be watchful and listening, that our obedience to God will lead us *"on the way"*—the way we have been told to go.

> *"You must not bow yourself [in worship] to [other] gods, nor serve them, nor do according to their doings, but do utterly destroy them, and thoroughly break their standing pillars. And you will serve ADONAI your God, and He will bless your bread and your water, and I will turn aside sickness from your heart."* שְׁמוֹת *Sh'mot 23:24-25*

The war between rebellion and obedience is fought on the grounds of worship... to whom do we pledge our allegiance? Yis'rael is given no options in this matter—there is no room for misunderstanding. Not only is she forbidden to *"do according to [the] doings"* of gods other than ADONAI, she is commanded to *"utterly destroy them."* If Yis'rael is to serve ADONAI alone, there must be no trace of false gods in her midst—only ADONAI may be the recipient of her obeisance.

As disciples of Messiah, we allow far too many "gods" in our lives—not only failing to *"utterly destroy them,"* but actually offering them a place to stay. Let us take a long, hard look at the "gods" which receive our time, energy and devotion, and then *"thoroughly break their standing pillars"* in our lives. Blessing from ADONAI awaits us in full, but only if we will completely divest ourselves of the *"[other] gods"* we serve instead.

> *"And* מֹשֶׁה, *Moshe came in and recounted to the people all the words of ADONAI, and all the judgments, and all the people answered [with] one voice, and said, 'All the words which ADONAI has spoken, we [will] do.... All that which ADONAI has*

spoken, we [will] do, and obey.' And מֹשֶׁה, Moshe
took the blood and sprinkled [it] on the people,
and said, 'Behold, the blood of the covenant which
ADONAI has made with you, concerning these
things.'" שְׁמוֹת Sh'mot 24:3, 7-8

Our fathers swore an oath to ADONAI—without
coercion, they obligated themselves to *"do, and obey"*
everything *"which ADONAI [had] spoken."* Have we as
disciples of Messiah not made the same pledge? Have
we not obligated ourselves to follow daily after the
Master? And yet, the question before Yis'rael remains
for us today: will the people of God keep their word of
commitment and honor Him with their obedience?

Though humankind is infamous for broken
promises, we have the assurance that ADONAI will *never*
go back on His word. Therefore, let us walk not
according to the weakness of our fathers, but in the
strength and resolution of Messiah. May we honor
ADONAI's faithfulness by keeping *our* word of
commitment and devotion to Him. Let us obligate
ourselves to *"do, and obey"* not just the parts we like,
but *"all that which ADONAI has spoken."*

☙ ❧

Lord God of Yis'rael, put Your Name in me that I
may *"do, and obey"* all that You command. Teach me
daily to be attentive to Your voice—and then to be
quick to bring You glory by doing everything You say.
Show me Your ways, ADONAI, that You may bring me
into the place which You have prepared. I bless Your
Name, ADONAI, and I literally bow myself before You
now... You alone are my God and King, and I pledge
myself to serve only You for all my days...

T'rumah

תרומה

Offering
שְׁמוֹת Sh'mot (Exodus) 25:1-27:19

"And ADONAI spoke to מֹשֶׁה, Moshe, saying,
'Speak to the sons of יִשְׂרָאֵל, Yis'rael, that they
[will] take for Me an offering; from every man
whose heart impels him will you take My offering.'"
שְׁמוֹת *Sh'mot 25:1-2*

For keeping His promises to Yis'rael and delivering her into freedom, ADONAI expects nothing less than total faithfulness. And yet, though He forbids the worship of false gods and idols, He does not *demand* worship of Himself. Rather than forcing love and adoration from His people, He presents us with the opportunity to give out of our hearts. He is not like our former oppressors who beat us into submission. Instead, it is *"from every man whose heart impels him"* that He receives our offerings.

As disciples of Messiah, our hearts should drive us to give ourselves to ADONAI without concern for what we will *get* in return. Though we trust that our God will not hold back His generous hand from us, may our giving not be tainted by our expectations. Let us pour ourselves out unselfishly—not strictly out of obedience, but because we are impelled by our hearts. In the end, we will be amazed to discover that no matter how much we give, *He* out-gives *us* every time.

> *"And you will put the* כַּפֹּרֶת, *kaporet on above* הָאָרֹן, *HaAron, and into* הָאָרֹן, *HaAron you will put the Testimony, which I [will] give to you. And I will meet with you there, and will speak with you… all that which I command you concerning the sons of* יִשְׂרָאֵל, *Yis'rael."* שְׁמוֹת *Sh'mot 25:21-22*

He could have chosen to be a statue of gold, or the figure of a bird, or the carved trunk of a tree. But unlike the gods of this world who are forged by the imaginings of human minds and hands, the living, moving God of Yis'rael gives us His very real presence: *He* meets *us* where we are, and *speaks* to us by His own mouth.

How can we help but respond to a God who gives so much of Himself—how can we give Him anything but praise!?! ADONAI chooses to interact with His creation, not leaving us to guess if He is real or not. He does not stare back at us blankly as we give hollow obeisance to His inanimate figure. Instead, our hearts are drawn to Him because He actively moves us by His presence.

May the reality of our invisible God overpower us, as it crushes all our religious presumptions. Let us no longer treat ADONAI as the standoffish façade of an unknowable deity, but instead join Him in the interaction that He so welcomes and deserves. ADONAI is alive in front of us and inside us. Shouldn't we respond to the presence of the living God by giving Him our very lives?

> *"And you will make a veil of blue, purple, scarlet, and twined linen—the work of a designer—*

he [will] make it with כְּרֻבִים, *k'ruviym.... And
you will make a covering for the opening of the
tent—blue, purple, scarlet, and twined linen—
[the] work of an embroiderer."* שְׁמוֹת *Sh'mot
26:31,36*

Made in the image of the Creator—the Designer—
we were born to express ourselves through the act of
creation. Left to ourselves, we will fashion our own
idols and gods, quickly forgetting the One who made us
from nothing. In the broad strokes of ADONAI's canvas,
however, we have been given a framework to keep us
from coloring outside the lines. Once inside, we are free
to thrive according to the unique and creative wonders
He has made us to be.

In the delicate, beautiful tapestry of the *Mish'kan*,
ADONAI allows creative humankind to put part of
himself, contributing to the detail of the dwelling place
for the Creator. He has not locked us into a rigid form
devoid of expression, but is inviting us to take part in
His great Design. ADONAI provides the functionality,
but allows His *creation* to add the *style*. May we accept
the invitation and join the Creator in His magnificent
work, for He has given us the colors to be creative—
now it is up to us to weave the entrance...

જેન્ડ્રે ન્જી

Great God of Heaven and earth, I am in awe of Your
creation and Your presence. ADONAI, teach me to give
of myself to You freely and abundantly, just as You have
so magnificently offered *Yourself* for all that You have
made. Lead me into the fullness of life as I worship
You, the One and Only Living God. I magnify and bless
Your Name, O Lord, Designer of all things—thank You
for inviting me to help build and decorate Your house...

T'tzaveh

תצוה

You Are to Command
שְׁמוֹת Sh'mot (Exodus) 27:20-30:10

> *"And you—you are to command the sons of*
> יִשְׂרָאֵל, *Yis'rael, and they [will] bring to you pure*
> *beaten olive oil for the light, to cause the lamp to*
> *burn continually."* שְׁמוֹת *Sh'mot 27:20*

The lamp of holiness is pure and true… as should
be the fuel that supplies it. On fire for ADONAI, it burns
the oil that is free from impurity, casting the light of
unfailing brilliance. But even more than that, the oil—
"pure" and *"beaten"*—*"cause[s] the lamp to burn
continually."* Without ceasing, it illuminates everything
in its presence, calling to consecration all things upon
which its light falls.

As disciples of Messiah, we are called to shine that
bright, unwavering, eternal light. Like Him, we too
need to be *"beaten"* and *"pure,"* that our lamps will be
forever supplied by oil devoid of all contamination.
May ADONAI find us on fire for Him forever—our lives
ablaze for the message of His salvation alone. Let us
diligently feed the embers of our hearts with oil that is
pure and undefiled, that the flames of our devotion may
go up before ADONAI our God—and our lives *"burn
continually"* for Him…

*"As a jeweler engraves a signet, you will
engrave the two stones according to the names of
the sons of יִשְׂרָאֵל, Yis'rael.... You will put the two
stones on the shoulder pieces of הָאֵפֹד, HaEfod, as
stones of memorial for the sons of יִשְׂרָאֵל, Yis'rael.
And אַהֲרוֹן, A'haron will bear their names before
ADONAI on his two shoulders for a memorial."*
שְׁמוֹת *Sh'mot 28:11-12*

To perpetually stand before ADONAI on behalf of
His people demands no less than total consecration.
For A'haron and his sons, this meant not only a change
in heart, but a change of clothes as well—an ensemble
unique among all the garments of Yis'rael. It would be
upon A'haron's shoulders that the name-stones of
Yis'rael would be placed *"for a memorial."* As *cohen,*
the people were A'haron's burden to bear...

Should *our* burden be any less?

As *cohen forever,* the Messiah Yeshua stands
perpetually before ADONAI, having eternally taken upon
His shoulders the burden of the sons of Yis'rael. For the
nations, too, He carries the yoke of intercession—
blamelessly, He ministers to the Father in complete
holiness. As those who follow Messiah, can we do any
less than share the burden of restoring God's people—
even the whole world—to Himself? May the weight of
the proclamation of the Good News rest squarely on
our shoulders as we, too, minister to ADONAI on behalf
of all... consecrated to our God.

*"I will consecrate the Tent of Meeting and the
altar; I will also consecrate אַהֲרוֹן, A'haron and his
sons.... I will dwell among the sons of יִשְׂרָאֵל,
Yis'rael and will be their God. They will know
that I am ADONAI their God who brought them*

*out of the land of מִצְרַיִם, Mitz'rayim, that I might
dwell among them. I am ADONAI their God."*
שְׁמוֹת *Sh'mot 29:44-46*

In an unholy world, ADONAI chooses to make His
dwelling in peculiar places. The ordination of the
co'haniym and the consecration of the Tent of Meeting
created a pocket of purity which ADONAI could only
temporarily inhabit. But now, by the blood of the
Messiah Yeshua, ADONAI has a place in which to take up
permanent residence: the hearts of *men*. In this soft
machine, we are fully able to house the Creator—a holy
place for our God to call "home."

As pure and undefiled vessels for the indwelling
presence of God, we are no longer free to live according
to the ways of the world. Instead, we have been set apart
as ministers and meeting places for ADONAI—bringing
His presence to *all* peoples, so that He may dwell in even
the hardest of hearts. The One who brought us *"out of
the land of Mitz'rayim"* is waiting to bring us out from
our unsanctified ways. Let us be wholly consecrated to
ADONAI, so that He may dwell among us once and for
all—He, our God... and we, His people...

৵ ৶

Holy One of Yis'rael, I am smashed and beaten in
Your presence. Reform me as You will, God of holiness,
that I may serve You alone all of my days. Burn within
me, ADONAI; consume me and set my heart ablaze for
You! Teach me, Master, to share Your burden for Your
people—consecrate me, O God, that I may stand before
You on behalf of all. Thank You, Father, for setting me
apart for Your purposes alone. Dwell within me forever,
Creator of all things—I praise You, Lord, and bless
Your holy Name...

Ki Tisa

כי תשא

When You Take Up
שְׁמוֹת Sh'mot (Exodus) 30:11-34:35

"ADONAI said to מֹשֶׁה, Moshe, 'Go, descend,
for your people whom you have brought up out of
the land of מִצְרַיִם, Mitz'rayim have done corruptly:
they have turned aside hastily from the way that I
have commanded them; they have made for
themselves a molten calf, and bowed themselves to
it, and sacrificed to it, and said, "These [are] your
gods, O יִשְׂרָאֵל, Yis'rael, who brought you up out of
the land of מִצְרַיִם, Mitz'rayim."' And ADONAI said
to מֹשֶׁה, Moshe, 'I have seen this people, and behold,
they are a stiff-necked people. And now, leave Me
alone, so My anger will burn against them, and I
[will] consume them, and I [will] make you become
a great nation.'" שְׁמוֹת Sh'mot 32:7-10

With Moshe up on the mountain, it didn't take long
for the sons of Yis'rael to start looking for newer pastures
to graze. Quickly, they reverted to what they knew
best—the ways of Mitz'rayim—and... Poof! Out came
the newest god of Yis'rael. As disciples of Messiah, most
of us would never dream of turning away from ADONAI
and giving credit for our deliverance to another god...
at least, that's what we *think*. The reality is that we're
just kidding ourselves—we actually do it all the time.

Whenever we turn to the world for answers—or to our own strength to save us, or our old ways to comfort us—we are fashioning, bowing down, and sacrificing to other gods… and it is an abomination. ADONAI was prepared to extinguish the sons of Yis'rael, promising to *"make [Moshe] become a great nation"* instead. In other words, ADONAI *will* be glorified, even if He has to find someone else to do our job. Let us *"[turn] aside hastily"* from anything that would steal the glory due our Deliverer, and turn whole-heartedly to the only One who can ever truly save us.

> *"And [Moshe] said, 'Please, show me Your glory….' And ADONAI passed over before [Moshe's] face, and proclaimed,* 'יהוה יהוה אֵל, *ADONAI, ADONAI El, merciful and gracious, slow to anger, abundant in loving-kindness and truth, keeping loving-kindness for thousands, taking away iniquity and transgression and sin, but not entirely acquitting, charging [the] iniquity of fathers on [their] children….' And* מֹשֶׁה, *Moshe hastened and bowed to the earth and worshiped, and said, 'If, please, I have found favor in Your eyes,* אֲדֹנָי, *Adonai, let* אֲדֹנָי, *Adonai, please, go in our midst— even [though] they are a stiff-necked people—and You, forgive our iniquity and our sin, and take us [as Your] own.'"* שְׁמוֹת *Sh'mot 33:18, 34:6-9*

We beg with ADONAI to show us His glory—to make Himself known to us. But unlike Moshe, when *we* ask to see, it's usually because we're looking for *proof* that He is actually there. It's not enough to know that He's off on some mountain somewhere watching our every move. No, we want His undivided, personal attention, to hear and obey our every prayer *now*… or else! And yet, in His abundant mercy, grace and justice, ADONAI

stills His hand and does not exact punishment on us—
even when we have prostituted ourselves for the divine
affections of inanimate, molten veal.

The glory of ADONAI should send us face down to
the ground, not leave us posturing irreverently in His
presence. ADONAI alone deserves all worship and
honor, for only He can dispense justice—and yet He
shows mercy and unending *"loving-kindness for
thousands."* As disciples of Messiah, let us no longer
give ADONAI reason to show us mercy, but instead turn
aside from our stiff-necked ways as we receive His
forgiveness for our iniquity and our sin.

Like Moshe, let us hasten to *"[bow] to the earth and
[worship]"* the One, true, living God, that we may hear
Him proclaim His great and mighty Name. May we
witness the magnificence and splendor of His glory, and
once and for all receive His favor… as He finally takes
us as His own.

❧ ❧

O great and wonderful, mighty God, *"if I have found
favor in Your eyes—please!—cause me to know Your way,
that I [may] know You…."* May I no longer be an
obstinate adulterer in Your face, but Your humble,
faithful servant. May Your presence go with me, that I
will never turn aside and give my love to other gods.
Thank You, ADONAI, for forgiving my iniquity and sin—
for taking me as Your own even when *I* disown *You*
daily. Teach me Your ways, Lord, that I may never look
to my own means again. I praise You, ADONAI, for You
are always there. Now, *"please, show me Your glory."*

And (He) Assembled
שְׁמוֹת Sh'mot (Exodus) 35:1-38:20

"[And Moshe said,] 'Take from among you
an offering to ADONAI, every one whose heart is
willing, bring it....' And all the community of the
sons of יִשְׂרָאֵל, Yis'rael went out from the presence
of מֹשֶׁה, Moshe. And they came in—every man
whom his heart had lifted up, and every one whom
his spirit had made willing—they brought in the
offering of ADONAI for the work of the Tent of
Meeting, and for all its service, and for the holy
garments." שְׁמוֹת Sh'mot 35:5a, 20-21

For ten generations in Mitz'rayim, the only gods
Yis'rael had ever seen were still and cold—unalive.
Now, for the first time, the whole community of
Yis'rael was witnessing the feats and acts of their
mighty, powerful, and living God—the transformation
of a nation was happening before their very eyes. So
when they were asked by Moshe to give out of their
belongings to the house of ADONAI, the people
responded with the full force of their commitment,
gratitude and awe. "And they came in—every man
whom his heart had lifted up, and every one whom his
spirit had made willing—they brought in the offering of
ADONAI..."

Many times, we wait to give anything to God until we feel so moved. We wait to feel something in our hearts or for our spirits to leap inside us, prompting us to give to ADONAI. But we cannot expect to be lifted up by our hearts and made willing by our spirits if there is nothing in our relationship with God to which we may respond. Is your passion for the living God of Yis'rael a burning, raging fire inside you, or has your affection for Him waned—now still, cold, and unalive?

If we are willing to receive it, He is willing to transform us… before our very eyes. ADONAI is in our midst—we need only to open up and engage Him, and our hearts and spirits will respond and move us to give. Out of our belongings, let us bring every piece of gold, silver and bronze; and out of our hearts, let us pour forth praises, proclaiming with our hands and our lips the greatness of the living God!

> "And still the [people] had brought in to [Moshe] a willing-offering morning by morning. And all the wise men who were doing all the work of the holy [place] came each from his work which they were doing and spoke to מֹשֶׁה, Moshe, saying, 'The people are multiplying to bring in more than enough for the service of the work which ADONAI commanded to make.' And מֹשֶׁה, Moshe [made a] command, and they caused the proclamation to pass on throughout the camp, saying, 'Let not man or woman make any more work for the offering of the holy [place].' And the people were restrained from bringing." שְׁמוֹת Sh'mot 36:3b-6

So naïve were the sons of Yis'rael that they did not know enough to give simply out of religious obligation. They didn't know—as we know all too well today—that you're only supposed to give to God when duty demands it… and even then, it should be the absolute minimum. Like innocent little children who didn't know any better, the whole community of Yis'rael just kept bringing, and bringing, and bringing. Out of a willing heart, they brought their offerings to Moshe *"morning by morning."* Isn't that just *adorable*?

When we give to ADONAI, not only should it *not* come from hollow religious obligation, but it should be as abundantly and as often as we can. Imagine giving so much to ADONAI that we *disrupt* the workers of God, forcing them to leave their work in order to get *us* to stop!

Have you given yourself so completely to the work of ADONAI that you have to be *restrained* from bringing Him anymore? As disciples of Messiah, may our hearts be set ablaze—no longer cold toward ADONAI, but giving Him all that He is due. With everything we have and all that we are, let us give continually, abundantly and *passionately* to our God. Forgetting that we are crusty old believers in Yeshua, may we forsake our religious rigidity in exchange for childlike innocence… and *bring!*

ॐ ॐ

Abba, Father, help me to respond to You now, and pour myself out before You with an abundant and unstoppable offering. Forgive me, ADONAI, for waiting for You to move me when I should *already* be moved by Your wonderful love. I bless You; I praise You; I glorify and magnify You—awesome God of Yis'rael, You are worthy of all that is due Your Name. Teach me to shed my shriveled and blemished old faith, and be unashamed and unembarrassed to give to You in the youthful zeal that comes from Your salvation. Restrain me, ADONAI, as I bring my offering and everything I am to You…

פקודי

Numberings
שְׁמוֹת Sh'mot (Exodus) 38:21-40:38

*"According to all that ADONAI had
commanded מֹשֶׁה, Moshe, so had the sons of
יִשְׂרָאֵל, Yis'rael done all the service. And מֹשֶׁה,
Moshe saw all the work, and behold, they had
done it as ADONAI had commanded; so had
they done. And מֹשֶׁה, Moshe blessed them."*
שְׁמוֹת *Sh'mot 39:42-43*

Upon inspection of the Tent of Meeting in all its
glorious and intricate design, Moshe resolved that all
the work had been done *"as ADONAI had commanded."*
The place for ADONAI's presence had been prepared
down to its last detail—the meeting place was ready for
the Lord's habitation. Fire and cloud now had a home.

The construction of the Tent of Meeting was not
required for ADONAI to *lead* His people, but it *was*
necessary in order for Him to make His *dwelling place*
among them. As disciples of Messiah, it is not enough
to merely follow ADONAI where He leads—we must also
be as excellent in detail and design as the workers of the
Tent of Meeting. In the end, we too will be a dwelling
place prepared for ADONAI our God—a house He will
not just stop by to visit, but will come to live in... forever.

"...the cloud covered the Tent of Meeting, and the glory of ADONAI had filled הַמִּשְׁכָּן, HaMish'kan. And מֹשֶׁה, Moshe was not able to go in to the Tent of Meeting, for the cloud had settled on it, and the glory of ADONAI had filled הַמִּשְׁכָּן, HaMish'kan." שְׁמוֹת Sh'mot 40:34-35

One can only imagine the magnificent, awesome spectacle of the glory of ADONAI descending upon HaMish'kan. If ever the Lord adequately communicated His feelings to His people, this was it: You've done a great job; you did exactly as I asked—I approve; here I am! *"And the glory of ADONAI had filled HaMish'kan... and Moshe was not able to go in...."*

ADONAI desires to cover *us* as well—to fill *us* so completely that we are *"not able to go in."* We should find His presence so overwhelming that there is no room to assert ourselves—we can only fall under the weight of His glory. When ADONAI shows His approval by meeting us in the habitation of our hearts, let us yield our whole being to ADONAI, and leave *ourselves* at the entrance. Shedding all forms of self-ownership, may we *"go in"* in reverence... as ones who belong only to Him.

"And in the going up of the cloud from off הַמִּשְׁכָּן, HaMish'kan, the sons of יִשְׂרָאֵל, Yis'rael journeyed in all their journeys. And if the cloud went not up, then they journeyed not, until the day of its going up. For the cloud of ADONAI was on הַמִּשְׁכָּן, HaMish'kan by day, and fire was in it by night, before the eyes of all the house of יִשְׂרָאֵל, Yis'rael in all their journeys." שְׁמוֹת Sh'mot 40:36-38

The cloud lifts, and the fire moves... but are we willing to follow?

The sons of Yis'rael *"journeyed in all their journeys"* according to *"the going up of the cloud from off HaMish'kan."* Completely dependent upon the Lord, Yis'rael enjoyed ADONAI's clear direction, virtually unable to miss His cues. Where the cloud moved, they moved; and *"if the cloud went not up, then they journeyed not."*

Unlike the sons of Yis'rael, however, we as disciples of Messiah tend to wander where the cloud is absent and linger when it has left. Overly familiar with the indwelling Spirit of God, we are often deaf to His counsel and blind to His leading. The fire of God is a mere flicker to us, failing to hold our attention— because we are constantly gazing elsewhere, ADONAI is gone from *"before [our] eyes."*

Today, may our rootless, independent journeys end forever, as we rivet our hearts and minds upon the power and the presence of ADONAI. May we be so engaged with God—so enthralled with and attentive to Him—that fire and cloud would be rendered redundant in our lives. Let us heed the Spirit that is burning within us, that we may follow wherever He leads... stepping forward only when the cloud lifts, and the fire of God moves on.

෧ ෨

Almighty God, Inhabiter of lowly dwellings, come and make Your home in me forever! Lead me, O Lord, and I will follow; let Your Spirit fill me and guide me in the way I know I should go. Fall on me, ADONAI—fall on me with Your glory; crush me beneath Your weight, that I may forsake myself and live only for You. I praise You, God of my fathers, and bless Your holy Name, for You come near to Your people in cloud and fire, that we may know Your most excellent ways...

ויקרא

Vayik'ra · Leviticus

וִיקְרָא

And (He) Called
וַיִּקְרָא Vayik'ra (Leviticus) 1:1-6:7(5:26)

"And ADONAI spoke to מֹשֶׁה, Moshe, saying,
'Speak to the sons of יִשְׂרָאֵל, Yis'rael, saying, "When
a person sins unintentionally against any of the
commands of ADONAI regarding things which are
not to be done, and does something against one of
these... [He] will be [made] guilty—or [when] his
sin which he has sinned has been made known to
him—then he must bring in his offering.... And it
will be when he is guilty of one of these, that he will
confess concerning that which he has sinned...."'"
וַיִּקְרָא *Vayik'ra 4:1-2, 27-28, 5:5*

We know full well that we bear the guilt of deliberate,
rebellious sin. When we purpose in our hearts to defy
God or abuse our neighbor, we are aware that such
actions warrant severe consequences. But since we are
all basically good people—or so we wrongly think—we
judge ourselves to be *innocent* of sin. Because we do not
consciously *desire* to do wrong to others, we are therefore
not at fault... how can we be blamed for whatever sins
we unknowingly commit? It's just too bad that
ignorance of sin and being *innocent* of it are not the
same thing...

"When a person sins unintentionally... [He] will be [made] guilty." At first, this may strike us as unfair. Why should we be held responsible for something that we didn't know was wrong? We're responsible because whether it is purposeful or unintentional, sin hurts others. Guilt is therefore assessed not based on the condition of our hearts, but on the actions of our hands. Our motivation and lack of knowledge consequently have no bearing on the assigning of guilt. Mercifully, however, they *are* considered for the sake of sentencing.

The guilt for our unintentional sin is atoned for by the shedding of innocent blood and our *"confess[ion] concerning that which [we have] sinned."* When our sin is made known to us, we have only two choices: to multiply our sin by claiming ignorance as a defense, or to humbly accept our guilt, confess our sin, and receive complete exoneration for our crime. With mercy, our atonement is accomplished, and aside from some minor embarrassment, we ourselves are without loss. Innocence for unintentional sin can indeed be ours— not because we didn't do anything wrong, but because there is a Sacrifice by which we may be forgiven.

> *"And ADONAI spoke to* מֹשֶׁה, *Moshe, saying, 'When any person sins and has committed an unfaithful act against ADONAI, and has deceived his fellow [community member]... then it will be, when he sins, and is [made] guilty, that he will return [that] which he has taken violently away... he will even make full restitution, [plus] add to it a fifth [of its value]... and his guilt-offering he [will] bring in to ADONAI... and it will be forgiven him....'"* וַיִּקְרָא *Vayik'ra 6:1-7(5:20-26)*

Though we bear the guilt of our unintentional sins, their penalty is relatively lenient. But for any intentional and deceitful transgressions we commit, recompense is significantly higher. Such sins are *"violent... unfaithful act[s] against ADONAI,"* revealing the malice of the heart. A guilt-offering alone is therefore insufficient for forgiveness... *"full restitution"*—plus *"a fifth"*—must also be made.

Willful sin bears a price far greater than mere guilt—we become immediately indebted to it with considerable interest. May we be quick, then, to take this truth to heart: sin costs more than it's worth.

Let us rejoice that though our debt is high, there is One who is willing to foot the bill. So here is the question: are we going to continue compounding our debt, or will we act faithfully toward ADONAI from this day forward? Though there is forgiveness for guilt, the ultimate cost of violent, unfaithful sin is worth *no* amount of ill-gotten gains. May we turn forever from our iniquity and be only indebted... to the One who marks *all* debts—PAID.

ॐ ॐ

O Great God of Yis'rael, You are merciful, kind, forgiving and just! I praise You, ADONAI, for You do not leave me to heap more sin upon myself, but have provided a Way for me to be completely released from the painful obligation of my guilt. Judge and Redeemer, how can I ever thank You enough for eliminating the arrears on my account, and declaring me innocent of all charges? I bless Your Name, O God, and I am forever in Your debt—a price that I can easily afford, and am more than willing to pay...

צו

Command
וַיִּקְרָא Vayik'ra (Leviticus) 6:8(6:1)-8:36

"And this is the תּוֹרָה, Torah of the sacrifice
of the peace-offerings which one *brings near to*
ADONAI: *if for a* תּוֹדָה, *todah he brings it near...*
in the day of his offering it is [to be] eaten—he
must not leave [any] of it until morning. But if
the sacrifice of his offering is a vow or free-will
offering, in the day of his bringing near his
sacrifice it is [to be] eaten, and on the next day
the remainder of it [may] also be eaten. Yet the
remainder... on the third day [must] be burned
with fire...." וַיִּקְרָא *Vayik'ra 7:11-12, 15-17*

When the *co'haniym* consume a sacrifice, it's more
than just a tasty meal. To eat the sacrifice is to receive it
on behalf of ADONAI, and to render it and the giver
acceptable to God. In the case of the free-will offering,
the leftovers may be eaten up to the third day following
the sacrifice. But the offering brought near to ADONAI
as a way of saying "Todah! Thank you!" must be eaten
without delay.

The haste with which the thank-offering is to be
consumed speaks to how quickly we ought to give
ADONAI our thanks. When we come before the Lord,

hearts overflowing with thankfulness, He immediately accepts everything we have to give. May we, in turn, not be slow to give to ADONAI all our "todah"—for *He* is not slow to give to *us* so much for which to be thankful.

> *"And [Moshe] brought near the second ram, a ram of the consecrations, and... slaughtered it and took of its blood, and put [it] on the tip of the right ear of* אַהֲרֹן, *A'haron, and on the thumb of his right hand, and on the big toe of his right foot...."* וַיִּקְרָא *Vayik'ra 8:22-24*

In preparation for his ordination, A'haron was adorned with the priestly garments. With deliberate attention he was clothed—his chest, waist and head bearing the attire specially made for *haCohen haGadol.* And then, as if with no regard for this man's more outstanding features, Moshe slaughtered the ram, *"took of its blood, and put [it]..."* on A'haron's *big toe!*

We often think that as long as we deal with the more prominent issues of our lives, we will be sufficiently prepared to serve the living God. What we forget is that the tips of our ears, the thumbs of our hands, and even the toes of our feet all play a part in who we listen to, what we do, and where we go.

By overlooking the small, less prominent parts of our lives, we allow them the opportunity to exert their hidden influence. When we consecrate ourselves to ADONAI, then, may it be our whole selves—from the tips of our ears to the tops of our toes—dedicated solely for sacred service to the Holy One of Yis'rael.

> *"[And Moshe said to A'haron and his sons,]*
> *'And from the entrance of the Tent of Meeting do*

not go out [for] seven days, until the day of the
fullness, the day of your consecration—for seven
days He will consecrate your hand... and at the
entrance of the Tent of Meeting you [must] stay,
by day and by night [for] seven days, and you will
keep the charge of ADONAI and not die...."
וַיִּקְרָא *Vayik'ra 8:33,35*

With the offerings made and the *co'haniym*
sprinkled and clothed, the consecration of A'haron and
his sons had only begun. It would not be until the
fullness of one week that the ordination would finally be
complete. Day and night for seven days, they were
commanded to not go out from the entrance to the Tent
of Meeting; instead, they were to remain diligent in their
consecration, paused at the threshold of their destiny.

As disciples of Messiah, we too await our full
consecration as the Lord prepares us for daily life in
Him. Let us neither exit from His presence, nor
attempt the work of the ministry prematurely, but wait
at the entrance until our consecration is complete. At
the set time of our calling, may we be ready and willing
to enter—our lives fully prepared for His service. Let us
offer our hands and be sanctified in full, that we may
"keep the charge of ADONAI and not die...."

૭ન ન૭

Todah, ADONAI! Thank You for receiving the
sacrifice of my life! I wait for You, Lord God, for the
time of Your choosing, that I may enter fully into the
calling and destiny You have laid out before me.
Consecrate me, Lord, and make even my hidden parts
ready to be used in Your service. I give You glory and
thanks, Mighty One, for by the blood of Your Son, I am
set apart... sanctified for *You.*

שמיני

Eighth
וַיִּקְרָא Vayik'ra (Leviticus) 9:1-11:47

"And מֹשֶׁה, Moshe went in—אַהֲרֹן, A'haron also—into the Tent of Meeting, and they came out, and blessed the people, and the glory of ADONAI appeared to all the people. And fire came out from before ADONAI and consumed on the altar the burnt-offering and the fat. And all the people saw and cried aloud and fell on their faces." וַיִּקְרָא *Vayik'ra 9:23-24*

Having completed his consecration as *cohen* and his first sacrifices of atonement, A'haron accompanied Moshe into the Tent of Meeting. Who knows what transpired between them and the Lord during that momentous encounter—but when they emerged, Moshe and A'haron *"blessed the people, and the glory of ADONAI appeared... and fire came out... and consumed... the burnt-offering...."* Apparently, the meeting went well.

ADONAI showed His approval of Yis'rael's newly consecrated *co'haniym* by revealing His glory to all the people. In order to serve a holy God and approach Him on behalf of a nation, one must be made holy and set apart himself. As disciples of Messiah, we too must be fully consecrated and sanctified to serve the Living God.

Only then will He consume *our* offerings… and His fire and glory will be visible to all.

> *"…By those drawing near to Me I am set apart;*
> *and in the face of all the people I am glorified…."*
> וַיִּקְרָא *Vayik'ra 10:3*

Contrary to His command, the sons of A'haron had brought a *"strange fire"* before ADONAI. The swift consequences of that unholy act left A'haron in stunned silence—his sons were now lost to the all-consuming fire of God. An extreme response by the Holy One, no doubt, but it was effective in making His point. If it hadn't been taken to heart before, now it was painfully clear: *"By those drawing near to Me I am set apart."*

Our sanctification before God is not a one-time event, but an on-going dedication to holiness. Not only do we need to *appear* before Him consecrated and sprinkled with the blood, but our actions must follow—ADONAI's holiness demands that we do only as He commands. We cannot share ADONAI's presence if we are unwilling to behave in accordance with His holiness. May the fire of our lives be for ADONAI alone, that He may be sanctified and set apart—*"and in the face of the people… glorified."*

> *"…I am ADONAI your God, and you will*
> *sanctify yourselves, and you will be holy, for I am*
> *holy…. This is the* תּוֹרָה, *Torah of the beasts, and*
> *of the fowl, and of every living creature which is*
> *moving in the waters, and… teeming on the earth,*
> *to make separation between the unclean and the*
> *pure, and between… that [which] may be eaten,*
> *and… not eaten."* וַיִּקְרָא *Vayik'ra 11:44-47*

The standard for holiness is set by ADONAI Himself... and not only is adherence expected, it is achievable: *"you will be holy, for I am holy."* This is why ADONAI commanded Yis'rael concerning *"that [which] may be eaten"*—to teach us *"to make separation between the unclean and the pure."* That which is unclean, our mouths must despise; but that which is pure is already made ready for consumption.

ADONAI desires to consume *us* today—not with the flames of destruction, but in the fire of His holiness. He does not command us to be holy only for holiness' sake, but so that we may share His presence and be used by Him for His purposes. Pigs were never the point; rather, it is the lesson of purity and sanctification He desires for us to learn. As we minister before the Lord—bringing restoration between the Creator and His creation—it is our solemn duty to remain undefiled by the world. In every way, then, may we pursue ADONAI in all holiness... to *"be holy"* as ADONAI our God is holy...

ॐ ✎

ADONAI, my God, consume the offering that is my life—make me alive in You, that with my whole being I may serve You. Show me Your holiness, O God; send Your fire and burn me up, that I may be made worthy to humbly minister in the power of Your presence. As I draw near to You, may You be set apart and glorified in the face of all the people. Sanctify and change me, Holy and mighty God, that my life may be a living sacrifice... dedicated to Your service and Your holiness alone...

She Gives Seed
וַיִּקְרָא Vayik'ra (Leviticus) 12:1-13:59

"And הַכֹּהֵן, *HaCohen will look [closely at] the sore on the skin of the flesh... and [if] the sore appears to be more than [skin deep]... it is a sore of* צָרַעַת, *Tzara-at, and* הַכֹּהֵן, *HaCohen... will pronounce him unclean. [If it] is not deeper than the skin... then have* הַכֹּהֵן, *HaCohen isolate him... [for] seven days.... [If] the sore fades, and the sores have not spread on the skin... it was [just] a rash... But if the* צָרַעַת, *Tzara-at breaks out greatly... [and] covers all the skin... from his head even to his feet... [HaCohen] will pronounce him who has the sores clean—it has all turned white; he is clean. But in the day of raw flesh being seen in him, he is unclean...."* וַיִּקְרָא *Vayik'ra 13:3-4, 6, 12-14*

Is it a blemish? An abrasion? What *is* that thing? Apparently, it's a spiritual lesson masquerading as a skin disease.

When a person first notices that he has developed a skin abnormality, he is to go see the *cohen* for closer inspection. This is to determine if the person is clean or unclean—does he have a contagious skin disease, or not? Upon examination, *"[if] the sore appears to be more than [skin deep],"* there's no question—it's Tzara-at, and the person is unclean. But if the sore is only on the surface, it's difficult to make a diagnosis, and further observation is needed. Will it fade and turn out to be *"[just] a rash,"* or will it *"[break] out greatly… [and cover] all the skin?"*

Many times, our *spiritual* sores are *"more than [skin deep],"* yet we permit the disease to rage out of control. Since it is difficult to determine the nature of our own sores, we must welcome the eye of discernment and allow ourselves to be placed under scrutiny. It is vital that we not be oblivious to our state of health, for then we risk spreading our sickness. Only after close examination will our true condition be revealed, and an appropriate course of treatment be prescribed.

Sometimes, a rash is *"[just] a rash"*—but when we notice a sore, we need to not wait to get a second opinion. Even when everything looks manageable on the surface, the underlying problem may be much *"more than [skin deep]."*

"As to the leper in whom is the [skin] sore, his garments are [to be] torn, and his head is [to go] unwrapped, and he [must] cover over his upper lip and call [out], 'Unclean! Unclean!' He is unclean— alone he will dwell; at the outside of the camp is his dwelling." וַיִּקְרָא *Vayik'ra 13:45-46*

When we present with a highly contagious disease, our own personal cure is not always the immediate priority. Whether we are just slightly uncomfortable or in unbearable, excruciating agony, there remains the pressing responsibility to prevent further transmission.

Though disease and malady affect us on a deeply personal level, they do not relieve us of our duty to care for others. *"The leper in whom is the [skin] sore"* is not permitted to clean himself up (so as to appear healthy), but is to head *"outside of the camp,"* alerting passersby that he is *"Unclean! Unclean!"* As disciples of Messiah, how much more responsibility do we have when it is revealed that *we* are carriers of a *spiritually* communicable disease? We are not allowed to cover our heads and act as if there is nothing wrong.

In our former condition, contaminated by corruption, the Master welcomed us into His healing arms. But when we allow the sickness of sin to linger untreated—feigning uncompromised immunity—we become the perpetuators of an unholy epidemic. If our sores are continuing to fester, let us tear our garments, unwrap our heads, cover our lips, and head outside the camp. Love demands that we protect others by warning them of the infection we carry, even as we seek *and receive* the healing touch of Messiah—the only Cure for what ails us.

ҩ๏ ๏ҩ

ADONAI, my God, may I no longer hide my sickness, but seek complete restoration and total health in You. Teach me to no longer pretend that my sores cannot be seen—allow me no success if I attempt to conceal them from discerning eyes. Redeemer and Deliverer, may my recovery be a testimony for all who see me while I am *"Unclean! Unclean!"* O Holy One, please cleanse me— quarantine and reform me—that I will not spread the disease of wickedness and sin, but transmit the truth that perfect healing comes only from You...

M'tzora

מצרע

One Being Diseased
וַיִּקְרָא Vayik'ra (Leviticus) 14:1-15:33

"And [the one healed of Tzara-at] who is to be cleansed will wash his garments, and will shave all his hair, and will bathe with water, and [then] will be clean. And afterwards, he will come in to the camp, and will dwell at the outside of his tent seven days. And it will be, on the seventh day, he [will again] shave all his hair—his head, and his beard, and his eyebrows, even all his hair he will shave—and he will [again] wash his garments, and will bathe his flesh with water, and [he] will be clean. And on the eighth day he [will] take [his offerings]... And הַכֹּהֵן, HaCohen will make the sin-offering, and will make atonement for him... and he will be clean." וַיִּקְרָא *Vayik'ra 14:8-10, 19-20*

Alone, outside the camp, the one who has contracted Tzara-at remains isolated until the time of his healing. The *cohen* eventually visits the man, and upon seeing that he is healed, begins the process of cleansing and reintegration which will restore him as a member in good health among the whole community of Yis'rael.

In order to erase all remnants of the disease so that he may be considered *"clean,"* the one healed of Tzara-at thoroughly washes his clothes, takes a bath, and shaves off every single strand of hair. Though now allowed back in the camp, he is nevertheless prohibited from entering his *own house*—it remains off limits; he *"will dwell at the outside of his tent."* After seven additional days—and more washing, bathing and shaving—he is again considered *"clean,"* though his restoration is *still* incomplete. Finally, on the eighth day, he brings his sin-offering to the *cohen*—blood is shed, atonement is made, and one last time, he is pronounced *"clean."*

As disciples of Messiah, we too are considered *"clean"* by virtue of the shedding of the innocent blood of the Lamb on our behalf—but that is only the beginning of our restoration. Just as the man healed from Tzara-at had to be thoroughly washed and every bit of hair on his body removed, so must we be stripped of the remnants of death and disease we still carry before we can be fully restored to our dwelling place inside the camp.

Like the man healed of Tzara-at, we may also have to go through times of homelessness, discomfort, cleansing and sacrifice in order to be rid of the vestiges of sin from which we have already been saved. Though we have received our healing and deliverance in full, let us be eager to enter our dwelling place forever by first enduring the process of purification, so that once and for all, we *"will be clean."*

> *"And you will separate the sons of* יִשְׂרָאֵל, *Yis'rael from their uncleanness, and they [will] die not in their uncleanness, in their defiling* מִשְׁכָּנִי, *Mish'kaniy which is in their midst."* וַיִּקְרָא *Vayik'ra 15:31*

Though uncleanness demands our temporary separation from the presence of God, becoming unclean is an unavoidable fact of life. Be it through lawful or everyday contact between people, or *un*lawful and base self-defilement, we will all become unclean sometime... one way or another. The question is: will we allow *our* impurity to defile the *Lord* in turn? Will we approach Him without adequate separation from the profane thing that has made us unclean?

What is defiling you today? Whatever it is, now is the time to *"separate... from [your] uncleanness,"* that you may securely enter His perfect, holy presence. Exposing the Lord to our impurity and contamination is not an option—we must cast off all defilement so that we will *"die not in [our] uncleanness."* Let us separate ourselves from all that which makes us unclean, and come before ADONAI in reverent fear... separated from that which defiles... separated to His holiness—His clean and perfect holiness *"which is in [our] midst."*

ॐ ॐ

ADONAI, God of Yis'rael, sanctified and Holy One, I only want to bless You in the abundance of Your presence. Pronounce me *"clean,"* O God, that I may approach You in reverent fear—that I may bow before You free from all that profanes and defiles. Show me Your ways, O Lord, and help me to separate from the uncleanness I have heaped upon myself. Restore me, Father, that I may dwell forever in the sanctity of Your midst—in holiness I will come to You, with all uncleanness cast aside...

Ach'arei Mot

אחרי מות

After the Death
וַיִּקְרָא Vayik'ra (Leviticus) 16:1-18:30

*"And ADONAI spoke to מֹשֶׁה, Moshe, saying,
'Speak to the sons of יִשְׂרָאֵל, Yis'rael, and you will
say to them, "I am ADONAI your God. According to
the deeds of אֶרֶץ־מִצְרַיִם, Eretz Mitz'rayim (in which
you used to live), do not; and according to the deeds
of אֶרֶץ־כְּנַעַן, Eretz K'na-an (where I am bringing
you in), do not—and in their statutes, walk not.
My judgments you [must] do, and My statutes you
[must] keep, to walk in them... and live in them.
I am ADONAI."'"* וַיִּקְרָא Vayik'ra 18:1-5

The sons of Yis'rael were headed for the Promised
Land. After centuries of captivity and living *"according
to the deeds of Eretz Mitz'rayim,"* Yis'rael was now being
prepared to possess the territory of K'na-an—the land
of abundance promised to our ancestor Av'raham. So
what made this new land so much better—so different
than the land of Mitz'rayim *"in which [they] used to live"*?
Nothing. The people of K'na-an and their practices were
just as base, just as abominable, as those of Mitz'rayim...
and this is where ADONAI was *"bringing [them] in."*

Why would the Lord do this? With K'na-an no
better than Mitz'rayim, what hope did Yis'rael have for

a better life? *"My judgments you [must] do, and My statutes you [must] keep, to walk in them... and live...."* Reaching the Promised Land was not the only point— Yis'rael also had to *"do not"* according to the ways of life both behind and before them. The difference between Mitz'rayim and K'na-an would not be the land itself, but the *people* of Yis'rael—they themselves needed to change... to keep ADONAI's ways and *"walk in them."*

The Promised Land is not some magical place that makes all our problems disappear once we "arrive." By sheer nature, if we do not live by the laws of ADONAI, we will live by the laws of the land. As disciples of Messiah, we have been redeemed and set free from "Mitz'rayim"— but to truly inherit the Land and live the abundant life of Messiah *now*, we must *"do not"* according to our old ways. He is *"bringing [us] in"* to the good land promised to us, so let us dedicate ourselves to *"do"* all that ADONAI commands, that we may thrive in the Land *"and live..."*

> *"You are not [to be] defiled with all these [sexual perversions], for by all these have the nations which I am sending away from before you been defiled. And the land [itself] became defiled, and... vomited out its inhabitants. And [so] you— you will keep My statutes and My judgments, and do not any of all these abominations... [so that] the land will not vomit you out.... Keep My charge... and you will not defile yourselves with them. I am ADONAI...."* וַיִּקְרָא *Vayik'ra 18:24-30*

Not for lying or stealing, not even for murder or worshipping other gods—the nations who inhabited K'na-an were *"[sent] away"* and *"vomited out"* of the land because of sexual perversion. Deviant sexual acts are the very *"abominations"* that Yis'rael was explicitly commanded to avoid *"[so that] the land [would] not*

vomit [Yis'rael] out" as well. Apparently, sexual sin—
compared to other sins—is so abhorrently wrong that it
results in the dispersion and expulsion of nations. But
why bother issuing a warning against that which God's
redeemed would *surely* have no inclination?

As human beings, we should find these deeds
loathsome and disgusting in and of themselves, and
shouldn't need to be told that they are detestable and
vile. And yet, ADONAI *never* instructs us to rely on the
direction or guidance of our own moral compass and
convictions. For Yis'rael—and all of God's redeemed—
there was only *one way* that they would not suffer the
fate of the Land's former occupants: *"keep My statutes
and My judgments, and do not* any *of all these
abominations."*

Left to ourselves, our "morals" will *always* erode into
depravity, and what we ought to perceive as perverse
will seem to us as innocuous as a choice of lifestyle. Let
us, therefore, *"keep [His] charge"* and *"not defile
[ourselves],"* but adhere to the unwavering standards
and virtues of a Holy God, that we may withstand the
allure of every kind of detestable and unwholesome act.

ॐ ॐ

O Holy God, in my flesh I am perverse and
degenerate—do not leave me alone to my unnatural
ways. I praise You, ADONAI, for upon Your path I am
made whole—I am created new and unstained… a holy
vessel worthy to be used by You. Thank You, Lord, for
changing me forever, that I may not be bound by the sin
that is behind or before me. I bless Your holy Name,
ADONAI, for You are preparing me to possess the
Promised Land—a land where I will not be lured away
by the world, but ensnared only by the goodness of
Your truth…

Holy Ones
וַיִּקְרָא **Vayik'ra (Leviticus) 19:1-20:27**

"And in your reaping the harvest of your land,
do not completely reap the side [edges] of your
field, and the gleaning of your harvest [left behind
by the reapers] do not gather, and your vineyard
do not glean [what you missed the first time], even
the fallen fruit of your vineyard do not gather. To
the poor and to the sojourner you will leave them.
I am ADONAI your God." וַיִּקְרָא *Vayik'ra 19:9-10*

An abundant harvest is a blessing from ADONAI—by
it He displays His approval and acceptance of us. Every
piece of fruit, every kernel of grain, then, is the evidence
of and reward for our labor. Unfortunately, we tend to
treat the harvest as if it was something we *deserved*
rather than a blessing we were generously *given.*

Like locusts devouring a crop, we plunder the land,
ravaging it for ourselves. The harvest is no longer a
blessing, but now only a paycheck—each morsel
representing a portion of a meal or a shekel at the
market. Either out of fear or greed, we expend
ourselves to amass every scrap and speck—fear, that we
won't see another harvest like this again; or greed,

because *we earned* this harvest… it *belongs* to us, and we're *taking* what's ours.

All too often, we fail to remember that not everything God gives us *belongs* to us—at least part of it is intended for someone else. Though the *"side of [the] field"* is ours to reap, and *"the fallen fruit of [the] vineyard"* is ours to gather, we are to *"leave them"* for others to collect—we are quite rich and secure enough without them!

When ADONAI provides for us, it is always exactly what we need—even when we feel like we're coming up short. There's no reason to go back to the vineyard to glean the miniscule amount we missed the first time. Leave the portion that doesn't belong to you and gather only what you can carry at once—then watch the harvest become more than enough as ADONAI reaps a harvest in you.

> *"And when you come in to the Land, and have planted all kinds of trees for food, then you will reckon as uncircumcised its fruit. Three years it is [to be] to you uncircumcised—it is not [to be] eaten. And in the fourth year all its fruit will be holy—praises for ADONAI. And in the fifth year, you may eat its fruit—to add to you its increase. I am ADONAI your God."* וַיִּקְרָא *Vayik'ra 19:23-25*

The trees that we planted have yielded their fruit—they are all ripe for the picking. We reach up and take the choicest of samples, poised to taste the fruit of our labor. But though we salivate at the sight, anticipating the pleasure of that first, delightful bite, we are instead told to put it down. This food will not be satisfying our hunger today—all we may do is gaze upon its succulence and beauty as it falls to the ground, apparently, in vain.

Just because we can see the fruit, this doesn't mean that it's time to eat. Sometimes we have to bear that fruit again and again before we're even permitted to bring it before the Lord. Until the fruit of our labor is acceptable and dedicated to God, we are to *"reckon [it] as uncircumcised—it is not [to be] eaten."* Then, in the time of *His* choosing, we are to bring it before Him, that the fruit may be made *"holy—praises for ADONAI."*

When we labor for God, it's not up to us to decide when the fruit is ready. As we wait patiently for our crops to bear acceptable fruit, may *we* bear the fruit of patience, trusting that ADONAI will satisfy all of our hunger and desires. Let us not rush ahead and partake of the fruit before its time, but leave it untouched until it is made holy before our God. Then, let us partake of it with joy and thanksgiving, and carry away the fruits of our labor *"to add to you its increase."*

❧ ❧

Lord God, Creator of all things, may the fruit of my life be holy before You—praises to my God and King. Teach me, Father, to not treat the blessings of life as something I deserve, but the cherished fruit of a life wholly and humbly submitted to You. As You pour out Your blessings upon me, ADONAI, may they bless those around me in turn. O Lord, let all my laboring indeed be in vain if I labor not for You and Your magnificent holiness. I praise You, Great God, for You satisfy all hunger and thirst, giving the sufficiency of the harvest to Your laborers. I wait patiently for You to bear Your fruitfulness in me... in Your way... and in Your time...

'Emor

אמו

Speak
וַיִּקְרָא Vayik'ra (Leviticus) 21:1-24:23

> "And ADONAI spoke to מֹשֶׁה, Moshe, saying,
> 'Speak to אַהֲרוֹן, A'haron, saying, "No man of your
> seed—to their generations—in whom there is [a]
> defect may draw near to bring near the bread of
> his God... a man blind, or lame, or disfigured, or
> deformed; or a man in whom there is a broken
> foot, or a broken hand; or hunchbacked, or a
> dwarf, or with a defect in his vision, or eczema, or
> scabs, or crushed testes.... He will not profane my
> holy places....""" וַיִּקְרָא Vayik'ra 21:16-20, 23b

Talk about politically incorrect! If Moshe were alive
today, he'd have to answer accusations of discriminatory
hiring practices for disabled *co'haniym*. I mean, come
on! Why should *they* be punished just because they
have a physical deficiency? It's not *their* fault, you
know. Just let the poor priest do his job! Who does
Moshe think He is, anyway, going around acting like he
hears directly from *God* or something...?

To our modern-day sensitivities, it would be
unforgiveable to consider someone with a handicap or
deformity "defective." And yet, *"to their generations,"*
no such "defective" descendant of A'haron's may serve

Yis'rael as *cohen*. What is ADONAI saying?... that the
offering of a crippled person is unacceptable? Not at all.
A person who is disabled may bring his offerings to
ADONAI in complete confidence—only the *cohen*
receiving the offering must be without *"defect."*

A holy and perfect God must be approached only by
one who is holy and perfect himself. In this regard, we
are *all* defective and unworthy to perform the sacrificial
duties. Thankfully, there is One who is holy and perfect
in every way. Without spot or blemish, the Messiah
Yeshua eternally approaches ADONAI on our behalf, so
that all our offerings will be acceptable to Him.

So, label me a "Reject for Yeshua"—that's verbal
abuse I'm willing to take.

> *"And ADONAI spoke to* מֹשֶׁה, *Moshe, saying,
> 'Speak to* אַהֲרֹן, *A'haron [and say...], "[Anyone]
> who brings near his offering... a male of the herd,
> of the sheep or the goats—nothing in which is [a]
> defect may you bring near.... Blind, or broken, or
> maimed, or with a running sore, or eczema or
> scabs... deformed or stunted... [its testes] bruised,
> or beaten, or enlarged, or cut—do not bring it
> near to ADONAI....""'* וַיִּקְרָא *Vayik'ra 22:17-24*

He's at it again! Someone call the Humane Society!

Not only does ADONAI's holiness demand that He be
approached in perfection, but the offering brought
before Him must be perfect as well. ADONAI cares for
physically challenged animals as much as He does those
that are exquisitely formed—the imperfect ones are
simply not acceptable to slaughter for an offering.

But there is One who is continually approaching ADONAI on our deficient behalf, and He has also laid down His life for us—a perfect and spotless Lamb. Let us be thankful that ADONAI accepts only a perfect sacrifice and refuses a damaged offering—otherwise, *we'd* be on the slaughtering block ourselves... Maybe "defective" isn't so bad after all.

ADONAI is extremely strict when it comes to the perfection required for His presence. Yet He does this not to be exclusive, but so that all of us imperfect ones will be *considered as perfect* through the indefectible service and sacrifice of our Master, the Messiah Yeshua. Hal'lu Yah, only the perfection of our *trust* is required to offer ourselves as a living sacrifice to God! Though we are defective in our flesh, may we be perfect in faith—pleasing, holy, and *acceptable* to Him...

৵ ৶

You are perfect in holiness, ADONAI my God, and I praise Your glorious Name! Though I am deformed, defective, and flawed in every way, You O God have shown me mercy and made a *new* Way for me to enter— uninhibited and unashamed—into Your presence. Thank You, Father, for sending Your Son, by whose sacrifice I am rendered without fault. I bless You, my King, for You are worthy of perfection... and yet You still accepted me...

ב'har

בהר

On Mount
וַיִּקְרָא **Vayik'ra (Leviticus) 25:1-26:2**

*"And when you say, 'What will we eat in the
seventh year, behold, [if] we do not sow, nor
gather our increase?' Then I will command My
blessing on you in the sixth year, and it will make
the increase [of your land enough to last] for three
years. And you will sow [in] the eighth year, and
will eat of the old increase. Until the ninth year—
until the coming in of its increase—you will eat
the old."* וַיִּקְרָא *Vayik'ra 25:20-23*

Every day, we sow into the fields of our lives. We
labor diligently so that we may *"gather our increase"* and
provide well for our families. The repetition of life
teaches us to rely upon that continual, uninterrupted
provision. But should the cycle be upset so that we are
no longer able to work, we begin to question the future,
fearing that our most basic needs will not be met.

The Shabbat year is a reminder to Yis'rael that for
all of our sweat and self-reliance, there is no provider
but God. Whether we labor ceaselessly day after day, or
work comes to a standstill for years at a time, ADONAI is
willing *and able* to perfectly provide. Let us trust not in
the work of our own hands, but in the tireless work of

our Father, who loves us. For all our sowing and
gathering, it is only by the *"command [of His] blessing"*
that we eat—the food of His hand alone sustains us, and
by it, so shall we live.

> *"And when your brother has become poor,*
> *and his [ability to support himself by the work of*
> *his] hand has failed among you, then you will*
> *strengthen him [as you would the] sojourner and*
> *[temporary] resident, and he will live with you.*
> *You [must] take no interest from him, or [unjust]*
> *gain... your money you give [may] not [be*
> *charged] to him with interest, nor for [great] profit*
> *[may] you give [him] your food. I am ADONAI*
> *your God...."* וַיִּקְרָא *Vayik'ra 25:35-38*

Though we ought to habitually recall that ADONAI is
the one who gives us our daily bread, it is our custom to
easily forget. So we take to looking for ways to retain
and increase the wealth we have, erroneously believing
that our storehouse is a stronghold against poverty and
want. We will take in a brother in need, but only with
the assurance that we can recoup any financial outlay—
and if we can net a little extra profit in the process, well
then... more power to us.

But an occasion to show love is not a business
opportunity waiting to be exploited. Instead of being
concerned about how we will pay our *own* bills, we
should *"strengthen"* our *"brother [who] has become*
poor," and let our Provider figure out how to spread the
wealth around. May the interest we generate come not
from the fear of self-preservation, but only from the
selfless investment we make in others. Perhaps helping
a brother in need *is* an opportunity to profit—a chance
to increase in the knowledge of the loving hand of God.

> "And if he is not redeemed in these years, then
> he will [be released and] go out in שְׁנַת הַיֹּבֵל, Sh'nat
> HaYovel, he and his sons with him. For to Me are
> the sons of יִשְׂרָאֵל, Yis'rael servants; My servants
> they are, whom I have brought out of the land of
> מִצְרַיִם, Mitz'rayim. I, ADONAI, am your God."
> וַיִּקְרָא Vayik'ra 25:54-55

Over the course of life, we can become ensnared by
our circumstances. Even for the sons of Yis'rael, poverty
was always a possibility, and there were times when a
man had to sell himself into servitude just to survive.
Though time may have presented him with opportunities
for redemption, it was only with the coming of the
fiftieth year that he would be assured of his release.

Yis'rael's poor are not kept from living perpetually as
slaves in order to fulfill some vague sense of mercy, but
because there is only one *true* Owner of Yis'rael—"*to
[ADONAI] are [they] servants; [His] servants they are.*"
The price of our captivity has been paid, but not just so
that we may be free—He redeems us from slavery that
we may be *enslaved instead* to Him. Let us rejoice that
we have now been released into *His* service… bound by
the love of the Messiah Yeshua to the servitude of the
One who bought us—our good and faithful *Master*…

భం ఆర

O Great and mighty Redeemer of Yis'rael, I praise
Your holy Name! Thank You for Your perfect provision
in all circumstances, for showing me the ways of
selflessness, and for setting this captive free! I am Your
willing servant, ADONAI, dedicated to Your service.
Remind me always that my protection and deliverance
come only from You—that trust in myself is in vain. I
bless You, ADONAI, compassionate and loving God—
may Your investment in me not return void…

B'chukotai

בחקתי

In My Statutes
וַיִּקְרָא Vayik'ra (Leviticus) 26:3-27:34

*"If in My statutes you walk, and My commands
you keep... I will put My dwelling place in your
midst, and My soul will not loathe you. And I will
walk habitually in your midst, and will become
your God, and you—you will become My people.
I... brought you out of... מִצְרַיִם, Mitz'rayim, from
being their slaves; and I broke the bars of your yoke,
and caused you to walk [with your head held]
upright." וַיִּקְרָא Vayik'ra 26:3, 11-13*

Not just a temporary visit, nor even an extended
stay—ADONAI desires to make His permanent habitation
among His people. Could there be any greater blessing?
And yet, such blessing does not come without a price...
there is one condition that must first be met. The cost
is our obedience—our whole-hearted commitment to
walk according to His ways—for only then will He
"walk habitually in [our] midst."

When we walk in obedience to the will and the ways
of God, we authenticate the liberty He has freely given
us. The *"bars of [our] yoke"* have been broken for a
purpose, that we may cast off all restraint and *"walk
upright"* in Him. As we embrace ADONAI's freedom and

wander not from His commands, He will savor the fragrance of our submission. Let us pledge ourselves to walk in agreement with His ways, that His *"soul will not loathe"* us, and we will find the path into His presence.

> *"And if... you [do] not listen to Me, and [you] walk against Me in hostility, then I will walk against you in the rage of [My] hostility, and I will even discipline you seven times for your sins. And you will eat the flesh of your sons; even [the] flesh of your daughters you will eat. And I will destroy your high places, and cut down your images, and will put your dead bodies on the dead bodies of your idols, and My soul will loathe you."*
> וַיִּקְרָא *Vayik'ra 26:27-30*

We joyfully hope for freedom and blessings when we commit ourselves to walk with God—unfortunately, the outlook is not quite as pleasant if we choose to *"walk against"* Him instead. The progressive gravity of ADONAI's warning should astonish us—the gruesome fate we face is astounding. In disobedience, we become nothing more than *"dead bodies"* heaped upon the idols we choose to serve in His place. We are cut down, loathed by God, suffering *"the rage of [ADONAI's well-justified] hostility."* The lingering flavor of familial flesh leaves a grisly taste in our mouths.

Let us heed the admonition of ADONAI, hearing both the exhortation and the alarm: count the cost and walk with God, or pay the price of walking away. In His kindness and compassion, He holds us to our vow—though He desires not to pass judgment. Rather, He longs to dwell with joy in our midst... just waiting for us to go His way...

*"And [if] they have confessed their guilt and the
guilt of their fathers (in... which they have acted
unfaithfully against Me and... walked against Me,
in hostility...) or [when] their uncircumcised heart
is humbled, and then they accept the punishment of
their unfaithfulness, then I will remember My
covenant...."* וַיִּקְרָא *Vayik'ra 26:40-42*

Should our eyes ever falter, our ears cease to hear,
and we heed not the warning of the Lord, we may find
ourselves crushed under the weight of our own
unfaithfulness, our bodies as broken as the yoke of our
old ways. And yet, if ever such ruin should come upon
us, ADONAI keeps safe the way for our restoration. The
question is, despite our condition, will we be willing to
bow low enough to reach it?

No matter how far we fall, if we *"accept the
punishment of [our] unfaithfulness, then [He] will
remember [His] covenant"* and preserve us. May we
forever choose to abandon all hostility toward God, and
instead bow our hearts—*and our backs*—to the One
who can restore our soul.

಄ ಄

Great God of Yis'rael, giver of freedom, resident of
my heart—You are just and graceful in judgment. I
praise You, ADONAI, for even in Your wrath, You will
permit mercy to prevail and grant restoration. Forgive
me, ADONAI, for ever walking against You in hostility—
forgive my unfaithfulness toward You, the Only God. I
bless You, Master, and bow to You in all humility—for
even when I deserve punishment, You forget my sin...
and remember all Your promises to me...

במדבר

B'mid'bar · Numbers

במדבר

In the Wilderness
בְּמִדְבַּר B'mid'bar (Numbers) 1:1-4:20

"And the לְוִיִּם*, Leviyim… were not numbered with [the others], and* ADONAI *spoke to* מֹשֶׁה*, Moshe, saying, 'Only the tribe of* לֵוִי*, Leviy you will not number, and their sum you will not take up in the midst of the sons of* יִשְׂרָאֵל*, Yis'rael…. Appoint the* לְוִיִּם*, Leviyim over* הַמִּשְׁכָּן*, HaMish'kan… they [must] carry [it] and all its vessels, and they [will] serve it….'"* בְּמִדְבַּר *B'mid'bar 1:47-54*

In all of Yis'rael, the sons of Leviy alone were not to be counted and enlisted in the army—to risk life and limb on behalf of the people; to put themselves in harm's way for the preservation of the innocent. Instead, they were called for a service even more gallant—more hallowed and sacred—than that of their brothers. The Leviyim were *"appoint[ed]… over HaMish'kan… to carry [it] and all its vessels… [to] serve it."* Yes, Leviy was set apart for the most distinguished, illustrious labor of all… manual labor, that is.

As disciples of Messiah, we all desire to be closer to God. What we often don't realize, however, is that the closer we get, the more of the *grunge work* we're likely to be given. Being close to God does not necessarily mean that we are offered more prominent or celebrated tasks. On the contrary, it means that He can trust us to work in anonymity, joyfully putting our backs into even the most menial of labor. May the Lord call *us* to such enviable work as *furniture moving*—to serve Him with sweat and by the strength of our hands.

> "And ADONAI spoke to מֹשֶׁה, Moshe, saying, 'Bring near the tribe of לֵוִי, Leviy, and you will cause it to stand before אַהֲרֹן הַכֹּהֵן, A'haron HaCohen, and they will serve him and keep his charge, and the charge of the whole community... to do the service of הַמִּשְׁכָּן, HaMish'kan.'"
> בְּמִדְבַּר *B'mid'bar 3:5-7*

Despite their high calling and position, the Leviyim would soon learn that a life of service to God was far from glamorous. Their special place of honor among the sons of Yis'rael may have earned them respect... but glory? Hardly. Instead of an elevated status among their brothers, the Leviyim were set apart as *servants*— their charge was to assist *HaCohen HaGadol*, and to labor on behalf of the whole community of Yis'rael.

Sometimes, we like to imagine that God has something more for us... something grander or of more renown than what we are doing with our lives right now. But if our hearts truly desire to serve God, we need to serve Him well *today*—to not dreamily neglect our duties and look beyond our charge. As His servants, our lives are His to do with as He wills. Our only job, then, is to dedicate ourselves to the service of our calling, seeking neither glory nor fame... but only *Him*.

> "And ADONAI spoke to מֹשֶׁה, Moshe, saying, 'And I, behold, I have taken the לְוִיִּם, Leviyim

*from the midst of the sons of יִשְׂרָאֵל, Yis'rael
instead of every first-born... the לְוִיִּם, Leviyim are
Mine, for Mine is every first-born... Mine they
are, I am ADONAI.'"* בְּמִדְבַּר *B'mid'bar 3:11-13*

Though the Leviyim daily bear the weight of their
selection, their service is not without its reward. For a
life of selflessness and sacrifice, a life of lifting and
carrying the burdens of others, there is this prize—and
it is no small consolation—*"Mine they are, I am
ADONAI."* By redeeming the lives of the first-born of
Yis'rael, the Leviyim themselves become the first-born
of God; owned by no one and no thing, they belong
solely to ADONAI.

As disciples of Messiah, we have been charged with
carrying the burden for all mankind. The question is,
are we willing to relinquish ownership over ourselves
that we may be used by God to give life to the world?
Out of all the people on earth, ADONAI has taken us for
Himself—but not for our sake alone. By submitting
our lives completely to His will, the loss of self will be
gain for others, and we will fulfill the sacrifice of service
to which we have been called. Is the price of our lives
too high to pay for the Master to call us, *"Mine"*?

&ᔫ ᔑ&

ADONAI, my God—I bless Your holy Name. May
my hands be calloused and my back be broken for the
sake of the service for which You have set me apart. I
praise You, Lord, for You do not elevate me in glory,
but glorify Yourself through my humility, as I give up
my life daily to You. I exalt You alone, ADONAI, and
praise You for choosing me as Your servant. Thank
You, O God, for taking me from myself... that I may be
only and forever Yours...

Naso

נשא

Take Up
בְּמִדְבַּר B'mid'bar (Numbers) 4:21-7:89

"And ADONAI *spoke to* מֹשֶׁה, *Moshe, saying,
'...when any man's wife turns aside and has been
unfaithful to him... and a spirit of jealousy passes
over him... whether she has... [or] has not been
defiled...* הַכֹּהֵן, *HaCohen will cause her to swear
[an oath], and will say to the woman, "... If you
have turned aside [while] under your husband['s
authority], and if you have been defiled, and
another man had his relations with you... may
these waters which cause the curse go into your
inward parts, and cause your belly to swell and
your thigh to fall." And the woman will say,
"*אָמֵן אָמֵן, *Amen, Amen!" And* הַכֹּהֵן, *HaCohen
will write these oaths on a scroll, and will wipe
them* out *into the bitter waters, and will cause the
woman to drink [them].... This is the* תּוֹרָה, *Torah
of jealousies, when a wife turns aside...."'*
בְּמִדְבַּר *B'mid'bar 5:11-12, 14, 19-20, 22-24, 29*

Most of us do not consider jealousy to be a positive
attribute, as it is generally associated with feelings of
inadequacy and low self-esteem. When we exhibit signs
of jealousy, especially as it regards a loved one, we are
told to suppress such feelings—that we are just trying to

be controlling or manipulative. But within the covenantal relationship of marriage, when a spouse is suspected of unfaithfulness, the *only* reasonable and healthy response is righteous jealousy: the overwhelming feeling that a sacred trust has been violated.

According to *"the Torah of jealousies,"* a husband has a right to receive restitution in the event his marriage bed has been defiled. When *"a spirit of jealousy passes over him,"* he is to bring his wife to the *cohen* for a remarkably unusual ritual. How her body responds to the mysterious concoction of *"bitter waters"* will be either recompense for the husband or exoneration for the wife—there will be no question of her guilt or innocence; the truth will be fully revealed.

At the heart of the ritual, however, is not just the faithfulness-potion the wife is required to ingest. In fact, she is to *"swear [an oath]"* that is to be written down... and *"wipe[d]... out into the bitter waters."* Forced to literally drink her own words, if she speaks truthfully of her purity, no harm will come to her—but if she swears to be innocent in the midst of her guilt, *"the curse [will] go into [her] inward parts."*

The oaths we swear—especially to those with whom we are covenantally bound—commit us to a relationship of uncompromising faithfulness. The vows we make with our lips are meant to assure the actions of our hands, so that we can freely and mutually give of our trust, and benefit from the happiness that such dependence brings. May we be faithful to our loved ones, that our word may truly be our bond, lest we nullify the integrity of our vows... and face the bitter consequences.

"And ADONAI [said], 'This [is how] you will bless the sons of יִשְׂרָאֵל, *Yis'rael, saying to them, "ADONAI [will] bless you and guard you; ADONAI*

[will] cause His presence to shine upon you, and
favor you; ADONAI [will] lift His presence towards
you, and appoint for you—peace." And they will
put My Name upon the sons of יִשְׂרָאֵל, *Yis'rael, and*
I—I will bless them.'" בְּמִדְבַּר *B'mid'bar 6:22-27*

Uncompromising, covenantal faithfulness is exactly
the promise that ADONAI makes to the sons of Yis'rael.
With His words, ADONAI obligates Himself to provide
for and protect His people—to bless them with His
peace and the abundance of His presence. Such an
oath is not made lightly and should be taken as an
unbreakable vow. Indeed, the word of the Lord is
spoken with the weight of dedication, the gravity of
commitment, and the solemnity of devotion.

Our word can be like that of an unfaithful wife
which goes down into the inward parts and brings a
curse, or it can be like the word of the Lord which
"put[s His] Name upon… Yis'rael" and yields eternal
blessing alone. Let us be jealous for the faithfulness of
one another, and in turn be motivated to remain true to
the covenants of our mouths. In this way our name will
never become a curse, but our word will be a blessing,
and our presence will shine our love.

ॐ ॐ

ADONAI, my God, Your Name is trustworthy and
true—Your word is Faithful, full of blessing and honor.
Father, seal the words of my lips, that I will not falter
through my actions and break the covenants of my
heart. Teach me Your ways, O Lord, so I will remain
faithful to those whom I love—that their love for me
will not be in vain. I magnify Your Name, ADONAI,
Guardian of Yis'rael, God of unending, everlasting love.

B'ha'alot'cha

בהעלתך

In Your Causing to Go Up
בְּמִדְבַּר B'mid'bar (Numbers) 8:1-12:16

*"And מֹשֶׁה, Moshe heard the people weeping…
and the anger of ADONAI burned exceedingly… and
מֹשֶׁה, Moshe said to ADONAI, 'Why have You done
evil to Your servant (and why have I not found
grace in Your eyes)—to put the burden of all these
people upon me? I—have I conceived all these
people? I—have I begotten them, that You say to
me, "Carry them in your bosom as a nurse bears a
[nursing] infant…?" For they weep to me, saying,
"Give to us meat that we [may] eat." I am not
able—I alone—to bear all these people, for it is too
heavy for me…. If this [is how] You are [going] to
treat me, [just] kill me, please; kill [me now] if I
have found grace in Your eyes, and let me not look
on my affliction.'" בְּמִדְבַּר B'mid'bar 11:10-15*

Sure, Moshe was being a bit melodramatic—but
with good reason. At his wit's end with regard to the
people of Yis'rael, he unloaded on the Lord in a fit of
exasperation. Perhaps this was not the wisest course of
action—accusing ADONAI of saddling him with a
responsibility worse than *death*—but as it turned out,
the Lord was pretty upset about the situation Himself.
While Moshe rattled on in his frustrated fury, *"the anger*

of ADONAI burned exceedingly." This is always a good thing to keep in mind when we're airing our grievances to the Lord: sometimes, He's just as irritated about our circumstances as we are.

Moshe had been given the near-impossible task of caring for a whiny, ungrateful nation. And though he did his best to provoke ADONAI into putting him out of his misery, the Lord wasn't about to suffer alone. Enlisting the elders to help shoulder the burden, ADONAI and His prophet Moshe would continue to endure... though they *both* had moments when they might have just as soon given up on the lot of them.

It should comfort us to know—especially when we have reached the end of ourselves—that ADONAI *does* feel our pain and, at times, identify with our struggles. Though we would always do well to watch what we say to the Lord, sometimes we need to let it all hang out with Him before He will send us some relief. We should take great care not to accuse ADONAI of being intentionally insensitive toward us, but it's okay to approach Him—every now and then—to see if He agrees that our condition is *for the birds...*

> *"Say to the people..., 'You have wept in the ears of ADONAI, saying, "Who will give us meat? For we had [it] good in* מִצְרַיִם, *Mitz'rayim." Well, ADONAI will give you meat, and you will eat [it]. You will not eat [just] one day, nor two days, nor five days, nor ten days, nor twenty days—for a month... [you will eat quail] until it comes out from your nostrils and it becomes an abomination to you. This [will happen] because you loathe ADONAI, who is in your midst, and weep before Him, saying, "Why is this? We have come out of* מִצְרַיִם, *Mitz'rayim!"'"* בְּמִדְבַּר *B'mid'bar 11:18-20*

Some might say that Moshe took a big chance by mouthing off to God the way he did—especially in light of what the people of Yis'rael got for their complaining: exactly what they asked for. The children of Yis'rael were stomping their feet and banging their fists on the table, bleating, "We want meat!" So, in His best parental form, the Lord responded, "You want meat? Oh, I've got some meat for you, all right... and you'll eat it *'until it comes out from your nostrils!'*"

ADONAI is pleased to give us everything we ask for—especially if it will make us eat our words. We would do well to watch our tone with the Father and show some appreciation for His generous and caring provision. Let us be slow to complain, quick to be grateful, and even faster to thank God for taking care of His own—thankful that as *"good"* as we think we had it in Mitz'rayim, we are far, far better in the Lord.

In tending to us, may Yeshua our Great Shepherd be glad that He gave His life for our *sins*—and *not* find, instead, that minding the flock makes Him *wish* that He were *dead!*

ഈ ഈ

Father, forgive me for all the times I have spoken to You like an ungrateful, spoiled brat! As I dump my frustrations out on You, Lord, may I never presume that You share them, too. I praise You, Abba, for Your loving, yet firm hand of care and correction. Thank You, O God, for giving me everything I ask for—*especially* when I'm really asking for it! I bless Your Name, ADONAI, because even though no one could blame You for giving up on me, You have never once left me alone... and according to Your promise, You never, ever will...

Sh'lach-L'cha

שלח-לך

Send For Yourself
בְּמִדְבַּר B'mid'bar (Numbers) 13:1-15:41

*"...And all the community [of Yis'rael] said...
'If only we had died in... מִצְרַיִם, Mitz'rayim, or in
this wilderness—if only we had died!' [To which
Y'hoshua and Kalev grieved...], '[Do] not rebel
against ADONAI, nor fear the people of the Land...
their defense has turned aside from off them, and
ADONAI is with us—fear them not!' And all the
community said to stone them.... Then the glory of
ADONAI appeared... and ADONAI said... 'How
long will this people despise Me? And how long will
they not believe in Me despite... all... which I have
done? I [will] smite them with pestilence, and
dispossess them....'" בְּמִדְבַּר B'mid'bar 14:2, 9-12*

The big, bad report that came back from K'na-an
left all of Yis'rael feeling frighteningly small. Soon, the
whispering became a thunderous uproar, and a spirit of
rebellion overtook the people. All they could hear from
the lonely voices of faith and optimism was a plan that
would lead to their certain destruction—they believed
all hope was lost. That was the last straw for ADONAI—
His already worn out patience was now completely
gone. If the people wanted to wish that they were dead,
then *dead* is exactly what they were going to get!

Wondrous provision in the desert, the miraculous feats performed in Mitz'rayim—even the prospect of milk and honey—these were not enough to sway the people from their fear and sin. If Yis'rael could witness the visible, manifest power of God, *and yet fail to trust*, how much more do we—who live in a day when such noticeable signs seem to be absent—need to disbelieve our eyes and trust in the unseen salvation of our God? What will keep *us* from rebellion but our faith? What will save *us* from our enemies but our hope in ADONAI?

As we face the giants of life, may we not despise ADONAI and enrage Him with our faithlessness and fear, but instead hold fast to the truth: *"their defense has turned aside from off them, and ADONAI is with us—fear them not!"* In faith, we must stand firm with the Lord and not allow panic and dread to lead us into defiance. The Land and its good fruit are ours for the taking. *"Let us certainly go up—and we will possess it; for we are thoroughly able to [do] it."*

"'...Please, now let the power of אֲדֹנָי, *Adonai be great.... Please forgive the guilt of this people, according to the greatness of Your loving-kindness.' ...And ADONAI said [to Moshe], 'I have forgiven, according to your word; and yet, I live—and it is filled—the whole earth—with the glory of ADONAI. For all the men who have seen My glory and My signs... and have not listened to My voice—they [will] see not the Land which I have sworn to their fathers.... [As surely as] I live—an affirmation of ADONAI—just as you have spoken in My ears, so I [will] do to you.'"* בְּמִדְבַּר *B'mid'bar 14:17-23, 28*

ADONAI's fury had reached its peak. Once again, Moshe made a case for the pitiful people of Yis'rael, and his appeal caused God's wrath to turn away... sort of.

ADONAI was ready to wipe Yis'rael off the face of the earth and start over with the sons of *Moshe*, but His hand was stilled and in His infinite mercy, He gave Yis'rael another chance. Moshe asked for forgiveness on behalf of His people, to which ADONAI replied, *"I have forgiven... and yet..."*

We like to imagine that when ADONAI forgives, He'll also forget to dole out our discipline. But not only does He remember, His correction perfectly fits our offense— and sometimes our own words become the template for our chastisement. ADONAI forgave Yis'rael according to His greatness and power, but the testimony of His glory demanded justice. By that generation's own fearful confession, they condemned themselves to a slow death in the desert—ADONAI forgave, but He taught Yis'rael a lesson *they* would never forget.

"According to the greatness of [His] loving-kindness," ADONAI does graciously forgive. Though He is not so full of wrath that nothing can appease His anger, He is also not so docile that we do not need to humbly seek His mercy. May we never become the engineers of our own end—testing the Lord and ignoring His voice. Instead, may we heed His word and see the glory of His Son—and know that as surely as ADONAI lives, He loves us... and all can be forgiven.

ॐ ॐ

Lord God of Yis'rael, Your mercy endures forever! Remove from my heart, O God, all fear and doubt, that I may instead see Your salvation, Your victory, and the good Land of Promise. Though I do not desire Your chastisement, I welcome Your hand of correction— restore me, Father, before my defiance rules me and I am lost to its wilderness. I bless You, Holy One, for Your justice and Your grace are good—may the words I speak in Your ears, ADONAI, be upright and pleasing to You...

Korach

קרח

Korah
בְּמִדְבַּר **B'mid'bar (Numbers) 16:1-18:32**

"And קֹרַח*, Korach... rose up before* מֹשֶׁה*, Moshe with 250 men... and they assembled against [him and A'haron, saying...] 'The whole community [is] holy... so why do you lift yourselves up above the assembly...?' And* מֹשֶׁה*, Moshe... fell on his face [and said,] '...Sons of* לֵוִי*, Leviy, is it [too] little to you that* אֱלֹהֵי יִשְׂרָאֵל*, 'Elohei Yis'rael has separated you from the community... that [now] you seek the priesthood, too?' ...[Then] ADONAI spoke to* מֹשֶׁה*, Moshe and* אַהֲרֹן*, A'haron, saying, 'Be separated from the midst of this community, and I [will] consume them in a moment!' [And Moshe pleaded,] '[When] one man sins... is Your wrath against the whole community?' ...[Then] the ground... swallowed [Korach]... and fire came out from ADONAI and consumed the 250 men...."*
בְּמִדְבַּר *B'mid'bar 16:1-4, 8-10, 20-22, 31-32, 35*

Furious that he and all of his generation were now condemned to the desert, Korach and his cohorts turned their rage and rebelliousness toward Moshe and A'haron. To justify his little insurrection, Korach shot at their alleged self-eminency, *"'the community [is] holy,'* so who do you think you are, standing between us and

God?" But Moshe saw right through Korach; his feigned concern for the people was just a ruse. What he really wanted was the position ADONAI had given to A'haron—the Korach faction was gunning for the priesthood.

ADONAI's response was swift and severe—Korach and his mutineers were swallowed up by the wrath of God. Indeed, the Lord was poised to obliterate every last Yis'r'eliy for Korach's sins—and would have done just that had Moshe not intervened. ADONAI established Moshe and the *co'haniym* for exactly this reason: to separate the people from God *for their own protection*. God forbid *we* should repeat Korach's fatal mistake and approach the Lord in unprotected arrogance... forgetting Who's *really* in charge.

> *"Then on the next day, the whole community...*
> *murmured against* מֹשֶׁה, *Moshe and* אַהֲרֹן, *A'haron,*
> *saying, 'You—you have put to death the people of*
> ADONAI...' *and they [assembled against Moshe]....*
> *And* ADONAI *spoke to* מֹשֶׁה, *Moshe saying, 'Get up*
> *from the midst of this community, and I [will]*
> *consume them in a moment!' ...And* מֹשֶׁה, *Moshe*
> *said to* אַהֲרֹן, *A'haron, '...Hurry to the community*
> *and make atonement for them, for the wrath has*
> *gone out from the presence of* ADONAI—*the plague*
> *has begun!' And* אַהֲרֹן, *A'haron... ran into the*
> *midst of the assembly... and standing between the*
> *dead and the living... the plague was restrained.*
> *But those who died by the plague were 14,700 apart*
> *from those who died for the matter of* קֹרַח, *Korach."*
> בְּמִדְבַּר *B'mid'bar 16:41-49(17:6-14)*

The people of Yis'rael must have been deeply moved by the martyrdom of Korach, their "champion"—in memory of his good and honorable name, they too rose up against God. Again, the Lord responded with rage, and before Moshe even had a chance to appeal, ADONAI unleashed His wrath upon Yis'rael in a storm of righteous fury. By the time A'haron tore into the midst of the assembly, nearly 15,000 Yis'r'eliym were already dead. He made the atonement and the plague was restrained, but what a price to pay...

Our imaginings of a loving, gentle God are not easily reconciled with this picture of violence and wrath. But our God would not be loving—nor would He be just—if He allowed the arrogant challenging of His authority to go unanswered. ADONAI was angry with all of Yis'rael when Korach despised the Lord, yet the nation was spared. But to witness God's judgment and *still* defy His authority—this was behavior that simply could not be excused.

How often do we witness destruction in the lives of those who challenge God, and yet fail to learn the lesson? As disciples of Messiah, we do not need to live in fear of ADONAI's hasty judgment, but we would also be wise not to flaunt the authority we have in Yeshua as if we are no longer subject to the authority of God. In Messiah, we have perfect protection from the advances of the enemy—but when the people of God oppose their Protector, who will be their defense... against *Him*?

જ઼ ઙ૿

Holy One of Yis'rael, Judge of all men's hearts, Your judgments are just, and Your wrath is poured out in righteousness. Search my heart, O God, and consume my rebellious ways—in holiness alone, ADONAI, may I approach You and not die. In humility, Lord, I worship You—may You alone be exalted in praise. Rip from me all arrogance and pride, that I may dwell in the joy of Your presence. I bless You, ADONAI, keeper and Protector—King of my life, Savior of my soul...

חקת

Statute

בְּמִדְבַּר B'mid'bar (Numbers) 19:1-22:1

"And there was no water for the community,
so they assembled against מֹשֶׁה, Moshe and אַהֲרֹן,
A'haron, and the people contended with מֹשֶׁה,
Moshe, and spoke, saying, 'If only we had died
when our brothers died before ADONAI…!' And
ADONAI spoke to מֹשֶׁה, Moshe, saying, 'Take the
rod and assemble the community, you and אַהֲרֹן,
A'haron your brother. And you will speak to the
rock before their eyes, and it will give its water, and
you will bring out to them water from the rock, and
will [provide] water [for] the community, and
their animals.'" בְּמִדְבַּר B'mid'bar 20:2-3, 7-8

Some things never change—the people of Yis'rael
were at it again! But no worries for Moshe—he knew
the drill: the people complain to him, he complains to
God, and then God gets mad and *zaps* a few thousand
Yis'r'eliym… no problem! And yet, something was
different this time. There was no anger or threat of fiery
wrath—in fact, it seemed as if ADONAI wasn't upset with
the people at all. Surely, Moshe was taken aback by this
turn of events. Rather than offering Moshe a
sympathetic ear and listening to him bellyache, ADONAI
told Moshe to *"speak to the rock"* instead.

The mouths of the people were spewing words of death, and now Moshe was being told to pour out words that would bring them life. ADONAI commanded Moshe to *"speak to the rock before their eyes... [to] bring out to them water from the rock."* Though Moshe was certainly irked with the people and might have preferred for *God* to deal with them instead, ADONAI's instructions to him were crystal clear. Just one question remained... would *Moshe* obey the word of the Lord, speaking only what he was told to say?

> *"And* מֹשֶׁה, *Moshe took the rod from before ADONAI, as He had commanded him, and* מֹשֶׁה, *Moshe and* אַהֲרֹן, *A'haron assembled the assembly in front of the rock, and he said to them, 'Listen now, O rebels! From this rock must we bring water out to you?' And* מֹשֶׁה, *Moshe lifted up his hand and struck the rock twice with his rod, and much water came out, and the community and their animals drank. And ADONAI said to* מֹשֶׁה, *Moshe and to* אַהֲרֹן, *A'haron, 'Because you did not believe in Me to sanctify Me before the eyes of the sons of* יִשְׂרָאֵל, *Yis'rael, therefore, you will not bring this assembly in to the Land which I have given them.... You rebelled [against the words of] My mouth....'"* בְּמִדְבַּר *B'mid'bar 20:9-12, 24*

Whether it was premeditated or completely spontaneous, we'll never know, but Moshe's abrupt soliloquy didn't exactly come off according to plan. Indeed, that poor rock was left out of the conversation entirely—not to mention getting whacked around with a big stick! Instead of *speaking* words of life to the rock and causing it to *"give its water,"* Moshe blasted the *people* with words of condemnation, striking the rock in what we may presume was bitterness toward *them*.

The people and animals drank that day because Moshe was fulfilling a directive He received from God. And yet, the ends did not justify the means—and Moshe and A'haron would suffer the consequences for *their* rebellion and lack of faith. ADONAI said to Moshe, "*You did not believe in Me to sanctify Me before the eyes of the sons of Yis'rael.*" Did Moshe not believe that he could get water from a rock by *speaking* to it? Or did he not believe that ADONAI made the right *decision* when He refused to punish the people for their incessant whining, and instead gave them exactly what they wanted?

We "*rebel... [against the words of ADONAI's] mouth*" when we hear what He wants us to do, but don't *listen* to how He tells us to do it. Moshe had made up his mind that there was definitely something the people deserved... it just wasn't *water*. But liquid provision was never the point—ADONAI wanted Moshe to obey Him by speaking words of compassion to the *rock*... not by rebuking the *people* out of the stoniness of his own heart. In his rebellion, Moshe still provided for Yis'rael—but at the needless expense of his future inheritance. He would have done better to set aside his *own* beliefs, and set apart the word of God instead.

ॐ ॐ

ADONAI, my God, may I go down to *sh'ol* with my brothers before I lift up my hand against Your holiness. Lord, Your word alone is faithful, just and true—teach me to not only hear the instruction of Your mouth, but also the desire of Your heart, that I may listen and obey. I praise You, God of infinite mercy, for You forgive even the hardest of hearts. Soften me, ADONAI, that I may know Your kindness and receive the promise of Your inheritance. I give You blessing and honor, O Holy One of Yis'rael, in whose word I believe and follow forever.

בלק

Balak
בְּמִדְבַּר **B'mid'bar (Numbers) 22:2-25:9**

*"And בִּלְעָם, Bil'am rose in the morning and
saddled his donkey, and went with the princes of
מוֹאָב, Moav. And the anger of God burned because
he was going, and a messenger of ADONAI stood
in the way as an adversary to him. And [as] he
was riding on his donkey... the donkey saw the
messenger of ADONAI standing in the way with his
drawn sword in his hand. And the donkey turned
aside out of the way and went into a field, and
בִּלְעָם, Bil'am beat the donkey... And ADONAI
opened the mouth of the donkey, and she said to
בִּלְעָם, Bil'am, 'What have I done to you that you
have beaten me...?' And בִּלְעָם, Bil'am said to the
donkey, 'Because you have made a fool of me....'"*
בְּמִדְבַּר *B'mid'bar 22:21-29*

Is Bil'am a good guy or a bad guy? It's hard to tell at
the beginning of the story. He's apparently in cahoots
with the king of Moav—so that's really bad. But he hears
from and obeys the God of Yis'rael—so that's really
good. At this point, all we know for sure is that talking
donkeys don't seem to faze him. Is Bil'am a prophet of
the most high God, or is he a corrupt sorcerer-for-hire
and a fool? Perhaps we should ask the donkey.

Sometimes, we need a dumb animal's perspective to see the stupidly obvious. ADONAI can be standing right in front of us—His sword drawn and His anger ablaze—and we don't even have a clue… we are so sure that we've heard God's voice, it never occurs to us that we may have *misunderstood* what He said. Each of us needs to get in touch with our inner-donkey—the part of us that's too simple-minded to know how smart we think we are. We would do well to listen to our donkeys every now and then, instead of beating them when they don't go where we lead. You never know… one day your donkey could save your skin.

> *"And* בָּלָק, *Balak said to* בִּלְעָם, *Bil'am, 'What have you done to me? To pierce my enemies I have brought you—and behold, you have certainly blessed [them]!' And he answered and said, 'That which ADONAI puts in my mouth—must I not take heed to speak it?'"* בְּמִדְבַּר *B'mid'bar 23:11-12*

Summoned by the king of Moav to curse Yis'rael, Bil'am's repeated entreats of ADONAI returned only blessing. Befuddled and bewildered, Balak confronted Bil'am, to which the enchanter responded, *"[I can only speak] that which ADONAI puts in my mouth."* Bil'am sought ADONAI for a curse against Yis'rael over and over again, but the only words braying from *this* donkey's tongue were declarations of exaltation and praise.

If the Lord can use even immoral fools to proclaim the wonders of His majesty, we would do well to not think so highly of ourselves—assuming that knowing God makes us more qualified to speak for Him. By opening up the mouth of Bil'am, ADONAI clearly established one thing: whenever He chooses to use people for His purposes, any old donkey will do.

"And [Bil'am said...], 'God is not a man—
and lies; nor a son of man—and changes [His
mind]! Has He said—and does He not do it?
And spoken—and does He not confirm it? ...I
see it, but not now; I behold it, but not near: A
star [will] come forth from יַעֲקֹב, Ya'akov, and
a scepter will rise in יִשְׂרָאֵל, Yis'rael....'"
בְּמִדְבַּר B'mid'bar 23:18-19, 24:17a

The same mouth that would counsel the women of
Mid'yan to seduce the men of Yis'rael declares the divine
character of God and proclaims the coming of His Son!
The same man who was hired to curse Yis'rael—a man
whose name is now a curse to us forever—was given
revelation of God Most High and foreknowledge of our
King, Messiah. Even upon the lips of fools may the
wisdom of our God be found... how much more should
we who *know* Him declare the greatness of His Name?

We cannot serve the will of man while proclaiming
the word of the Lord, or we too are liars and imposters—
deaf to the very truth we make known. May the word
that ADONAI puts in our mouth rewrite the end of *our*
story, so that anyone who hears it will know *exactly*
whose side we're on.

ॐ ॐ

Put the word of my mouth down deep in my soul,
Lord, that I may be a fool for You! Let Your word in
me broadcast the majesty of Your kingdom, that even I
will not merely hear it, but truly understand. Use this
foolish creature, Master—not because I am worthy, but
because You alone are worthy to receive all glory,
honor, and praise. I bless You, ADONAI my God, King
of all creation, who employs even fools like me...

פינחס

Phinehas
בְּמִדְבַּר **B'mid'bar (Numbers) 25:10-29:40(30:1)**

"*And* ADONAI *spoke to* מֹשֶׁה, *Moshe, saying,*
'פִּינְחָס, *Piyn'chas, son of* אֶלְעָזָר, *El'azar, son of*
אַהֲרֹן הַכֹּהֵן, *A'haron HaCohen, has turned back
My fury from the sons of* יִשְׂרָאֵל, *Yis'rael, by his
being zealous for My jealousy in their midst, and
[so] I did not consume the sons of* יִשְׂרָאֵל, *Yis'rael
in My jealousy. Therefore, say, "Behold, I am
giving to him* בְּרִיתִי שָׁלוֹם, *B'riytiy Shalom," and it
will be to him and to his seed after him a covenant
of age-enduring priesthood, because he has been
zealous for his God, and made atonement for the
[people].'"* בְּמִדְבַּר *B'mid'bar 25:10-13*

With each passing year, Yis'rael drew closer to the
end of her wilderness wandering—and with each passing
year, young Piyn'chas grew, watching his father and
grandfather serve an obstinate, immoral and adulterous
people. Piyn'chas agonized over the fate of his brothers,
as the influence of a fading generation continued to hold
sway over them. But when the young men of Yis'rael
finally succumbed to the seductions of Moav, Piyn'chas
could stand it no more. The blood of one Yis'r'eliy—
and his Moaviy harlot—would atone for the people…
at the lethal end of Piyn'chas' righteous zeal.

In the midst of a generation who had been trained only to obey the lust of the flesh, Piyn'chas stood as a lonely testimony to the discipleship of righteousness. By running the man and his mistress through, Piyn'chas not only satisfied ADONAI's justice, but sealed for himself and his sons forever a covenant of peace with God. The fruit of Piyn'chas' righteous upbringing was extreme zeal for the Holy One—and it was this zeal that would be his legacy until the end of time.

In every generation, ADONAI is looking to establish His *B'riyt Shalom* with those who would be radical fanatics for Him. Are we prepared to respond to God—to pick up our spear and drive it through our own? Or will we just look sorrowfully upon the sin of our brothers without the passion to stop the plague that is destroying them? Let ours be the generation willing to defend the holiness of our God! May we be zealous enough to spill blood for the sake of righteousness—and may the first life we take be our own.

"And מֹשֶׁה, Moshe spoke to ADONAI, saying, 'ADONAI—God of the spirits of all flesh—appoint a man over the community who [will] go out before them, and who [will] come in before them, and who [will] take them out, and who [will] bring them in, so the community of ADONAI [will] not be as sheep which have no shepherd.' And ADONAI said to מֹשֶׁה, Moshe, 'Take to yourself יְהוֹשֻׁעַ בִּן־נוּן, Y'hoshua Bin-Nun, a man in whom is the Spirit, and you will lay your hands upon him, and will cause him to stand before אֶלְעָזָר הַכֹּהֵן, El'azar HaCohen, and before all the community, and charge him before their eyes, and put of your authority on him, so that all the community of the sons of יִשְׂרָאֵל, Yis'rael will listen [to him.]'" בְּמִדְבַּר *B'mid'bar 27:15-20*

Despite the trouble and grief the people of Yis'rael had caused Moshe, he still cared deeply for their well-being—as a shepherd cares for his sheep. With the season of Moshe's life finally beginning to wane, he appealed to ADONAI to appoint someone new to take his place. ADONAI chose Moshe's faithful servant Y'hoshua—"*a man in whom was the Spirit.*" He was given of Moshe's distinctive authority, that he might lead the sons of Yis'rael in Moshe's stead.

For as long as Messiah tarries, it is our solemn duty to pass on to the next generation whatever authority we may have. The question is, to whom have *we* been faithful servants, and whose authority *is* it that we impart? Y'hoshua served Moshe with devotion and without complaint, taking no glory for himself. Can we say the same of how we have served those who have already gone before *us*? Eventually, we'll get our chance to be in charge—but will our life of service warrant such an honor… or will we just be the next generation who is simply not yet dead?

રે ન્ડ

For future generations, O God… for all those other than myself, ADONAI… accept my life as a living sacrifice! Lord God, fill me with Your righteousness, and cause me to be consumed with zeal for You. Ignite the fire for Your holiness in my heart, that I may be radical for the sake of Your great Name. Teach me Your ways, O Lord, that I may not stray from the path of uprightness, nor seek to serve myself and be left without a legacy for You to preserve. I bless Your awesome and mighty Name, ADONAI—fill my heart with compassion for Your people, that I may pour out to others even more abundantly than others have poured into me…

Matot

מטות

Tribes
בְּמִדְבַּר **B'mid'bar (Numbers) 30:1(2)-32:42**

"מֹשֶׁה, *Moshe spoke to the heads of the tribes
of...* יִשְׂרָאֵל, *Yis'rael, saying, 'This is the thing which
ADONAI has commanded: When a man vows a vow
to ADONAI, or has sworn an oath to bind a bond on
his soul, he must not defile his word. According to
all that has gone out from his mouth, he [must]
do.... But if in the house of her husband [a wife]
has vowed... and if her husband certainly says
nothing to her [about it] from day to day, then he
has [caused] all her vows to stand... for he has said
nothing to her on the day that he heard [about it].'"*
בְּמִדְבַּר *B'mid'bar 30:1-2(2-3), 10(11), 14(13)*

Some require a written contract; for others, a
handshake will do. But when we invoke the Name of
ADONAI—when we "swear to God"—our word is
literally our bond.

Truth be told, there is nothing obligating a man to
the generic promises he makes. Aside from a sullied
reputation and perhaps some sort of imposed penalty,
there are really no guaranteed repercussions if he breaks
his word. All that changes, however, when we make our
vows "*to ADONAI*"—suddenly, there is a reputation on

the line far more substantial than our own. To make
void an oath pledged in the Lord's Name *"defile[s our]
word"*—we have violated *"a bond on [our] soul."*

*"According to all that has gone out from [our] mouth,
[we are required to] do."* Be it by the word we speak or
the word we withhold, we *are* duty-bound to honor our
commitments. As those who bear the Name of ADONAI—
whether we actually swear in His Name or not—the
oaths we make are heard in His house, so *He* will cause
"all… vows to stand."

> *"And מֹשֶׁה, Moshe said to [the sons of Gad and
> R'uven], 'If you do this thing: if you are armed
> before ADONAI for battle, and every armed one of
> you passes over the יַרְדֵּן, Yar'den before ADONAI,
> until he dispossesses His enemies from before Him
> and the Land has been subdued before ADONAI—
> then afterwards you may turn back, and will be free
> [from obligation] to ADONAI and to יִשְׂרָאֵל, Yis'rael;
> and this land [east of the Yar'den] will be to you
> for a possession before ADONAI. But if you do not
> so, behold, you [will] have sinned against ADONAI.
> And know [for sure] that your sin—it will find
> you.'"* בְּמִדְבַּר B'mid'bar 32:20-23

The sons of Gad and R'uven were ready to leave the
people shorthanded in their impending battle for the
Land. Instead, Moshe compelled the men to fight
alongside their brothers until the Land of Yis'rael was
subdued. If they fulfilled this obligation, the Gadiy and
R'uveniy would be free to go back over the Yar'den,
settling there with their families in peace. *"But if [they
did] not so… [they would] have sinned against ADONAI,"*
and surely, their sin *"[would] find [them]."*

When we go back on our word, we had better be prepared for a life of running, because who knows what sin will do to us once we are found. A man of broken promises is like a fugitive trying to elude a relentless captor—eventually all his hiding places will be exposed, and he will have nowhere left to go. There is no safe harbor, no moment's peace. He has betrayed the integrity of his word—and now, there is no place for the prey to lay his weary head. A broken promise is a sin against ADONAI, and there *will* be consequences.

When it seems as if nothing ever goes right and we just can't get out from under the difficulties of life, perhaps it is because we have not kept our word—sin has found us, and we are under its thumb. The promises we have made and broken, we know them all too well. Maybe it's time to finally fulfill our obligations, so that we can go back and possess the land that we have asked for and been given. Let us cast off the restraints of sin and make restitution for the price on our heads. Then, may we walk uprightly in truth, free from the pursuit of our enemy... honoring the vows of our mouths.

જ્જ ૭

ADONAI my God, hold me to my word, that Your holy Name will not be defiled. Whether by utterance or silence, enforce the obligations of my mouth, that my word will forever be my bond. I praise You, Lord, my protector; let sin no longer pursue me. Convict my heart of the oaths I have made void, and cause me to make restitution to those whom I have wronged. God of Av'raham—Promise Maker and Promise Keeper—I bless Your honorable and faithful Name. May Your trust in me not be misplaced, for I have placed all my trust in You...

Mas'ei

מסעי

Journeys
בְּמִדְבַּר B'mid'bar (Numbers) 33:1-36:13

"ADONAI spoke to מֹשֶׁה, Moshe... saying, 'Speak
to the sons of יִשְׂרָאֵל, Yis'rael, and you will say to
them, "When you pass over the יַרְדֵּן, Yar'den into
the land of כְּנַעַן, K'na-an, then you must dispossess
all the inhabitants of the Land from before you, and
destroy all their imagery—yes, all their molten
images you [must] destroy, and all their high
places you [must] lay waste. And you will possess
the Land and dwell in it, for to you I have given the
Land—to possess it."'" בְּמִדְבַּר B'mid'bar 33:50-53

No negotiations.
No diplomacy.
No compromise.

Yis'rael was instructed to wipe out the inhabitants of
the Land—to completely obliterate them; to mow over
their gods and raze their high places to the ground.
Peace talks? Immaterial. Treaties and accords? Hardly.
ADONAI's orders to Yis'rael were simple and direct:
before you can possess the Land, it must be utterly
purged. Show no mercy. Take no prisoners. Lay waste
to everything—and everyone—that stands in your way.

Lest we be tempted to feel outrage or compassion—
that ADONAI is cruel and heartless; that Yis'rael is
stripping a completely innocent people of their
fundamental human rights—let us not forget that *our
feelings are irrelevant.* It doesn't matter who had it first;
it makes no difference if the current residents are a
threat to us or not. ADONAI said that the Land must be
cleansed—that we are to go in, possess it, and dwell
there forever—no matter what the cost.

Our reluctance to cheer on Yis'rael's ruthlessness is
the same reluctance we have to purge our *own* lives and
take possession of our God-given inheritance once and
for all. Toward sin, we must be brutal—toward the
flesh, merciless and cold-blooded. If there is any hope
of driving out the enemies we have given refuge, we
must be callous with *ourselves* and refuse to be swayed
by the naïve propaganda of peaceful co-existence.

The land must be taken. The land must be cleansed.
No negotiations. No diplomacy. No compromise.

> *"But if you do not dispossess the inhabitants of
> the Land from before you, then it will be, those of
> them whom you let remain* will be *for pricks in
> your eyes, and for thorns in your sides, and they
> will trouble you in the Land in which you dwell.
> And it will come to pass, as I plan to do to them—
> I [will] do to you."* בְּמִדְבַּר *B'mid'bar 33:55-56*

The directive from ADONAI is plain: destroy
everything in sight and possess the Land. But should
the people halt their advance and fail to drive out every
last occupier from before them, the consequences are
equally clear: those people will become a source of
trouble for you—and you will be in *big* trouble with Me.

Like an infection that is not fully treated, the remnant of a foreign body can cause tremendous devastation— and we dare not underestimate its potential. Do we not writhe in pain at the infliction of a mere eyelash gone astray? How much more will prickled thorns leave us thrashing about in debilitating, agonizing torture? With the anguish of removal even more unbearable than the unending torment of their presence, we eventually lose consciousness, anesthetized by the barbs of affliction. If only we had rid ourselves of them when we had the chance—if only we hadn't invited them to stay...

Once we allow sin to establish its stronghold, we are faced with the inevitability of two most unpleasant alternatives... either allow it to fester and ultimately succumb to its deadly effects, or consent to being restrained as it is torn from our members—ripped out in chunks of bloody, hemorrhaging flesh. *"If [we] do not dispossess the inhabitants of the Land from before [us], then it will be, those of them whom [we] let remain"* will be our ruin. Let us withhold the invitation and post a notice of eviction in its place. Now steel yourself, because the campaign for your inheritance is at hand.

ও৵ ৻৹

Let the battle cry sound, ADONAI, and I will answer; with the thirst for war I will fall on my enemies. Gird me up, O God, that I may not falter; endue me with might, O Lord, that I may utterly annihilate my foe. You alone are worthy of all blessing, honor and praise— You go before me in battle and return only in victory. May my enemies know no mercy from me—may they flee at the sight of Your strength. Eradicate me, Holy and Faithful One; I gladly invite the affliction of Your wounds, for in You alone are all my sins defeated— Savior and Shield, in whom I am healed...

דברים

D'variym · Deuteronomy

דברים

Words
דְּבָרִים D'variym (Deuteronomy) 1:1-3:22

"And I said to you, 'Be not terrified, nor be afraid of them. ADONAI your God, who is going before you—He will fight for you, [just] as all that He had done with you in מִצְרַיִם, Mitz'rayim before your eyes, and in the wilderness. There you saw how ADONAI your God has carried you—as a man carries his son—in all the way which you have gone until your coming in to this place.'" דְּבָרִים *D'variym 1:29-31*

As Moshe begins to recount a generation's history of wandering, out of the record emerges the essential portrayal of ADONAI: our Father. *"As a man carries his son,"* so did ADONAI carry Yis'rael, lifting them up and holding them out of harm's way while He fought on their behalf time and again. Deliverer, Protector and Guide, ADONAI parented Yis'rael with a hand of compassion and correction. He went before Yis'rael to clear the path ahead, yet stayed behind when they chose to follow their own road. Who but a devoted and loving Father could care for His children in such a way?

Our Father does indeed care for us, and as disciples of Messiah, we too are the recipients of both blessing

and chastisement. The perfect parent, ADONAI never
fails to discipline us exactly as the circumstances
warrant; and yet, His love is everlasting—never
withheld, always poured out beyond what we deserve.
May we in turn be such devoted children that we never
forget the One who is a Father to us—not an absentee
who leaves us to make it through life on our own, but
"ADONAI your God [who] has carried you…"

> *"And the* אֱמֹרִי*, 'Emoriy who dwelled in that
> hill-country came out to meet you, and they
> pursued you as the bees do, and crushed you in*
> שֵׂעִיר*, Seiyr—[all the way] to* חָרְמָה*, Char'mah.
> And you turned back and wept before ADONAI,
> but ADONAI did not listen to your voice, nor did he
> give ear to you."* דְּבָרִים *D'variym 1:44-45*

Against parental advice, the sons of Yis'rael decided
to take matters into their own hands. But when their
juvenile haste failed to produce the intended results,
they came running and blubbering back to Abba… who
promptly ignored them. *This* is a loving Father? It is.
Which is more loving?… to show disapproval—even
anger—toward a child's foolish and rebellious behavior,
or to encourage future disobedience by providing their
insolence a safe haven? Though a Father may want
nothing more than to immediately comfort and
reassure His hurting children, Love chooses the harder
path—the path that will ultimately bring healing.

When we fail to listen to the voice of our Father, He
may indeed *"not listen to [our] voice, nor… give [us]
ear…."* And yet, we can be assured that His love is
without condition—that He still hears our cries, and
will console us in time. We can take comfort in
knowing that our Father disciplines us *because* of His

unlimited love, and no matter the wrong we may sometimes do, it is *always* right to run back to Abba.

> *"For ADONAI your God has blessed you… He has known your walking in this great wilderness these forty years. ADONAI your God is with you— you have lacked nothing."* דְּבָרִים *D'variym 2:7*

ADONAI, our God and Father, *"has known [our] walking in this great wilderness"* we call Life. He pays close attention to our path—disciplining us when we lose our way, yet blessing us when we stay the course. No matter how poorly or how well we walk with Him, our loving Father provides appropriately at every turn. It is in this way that *"you have lacked nothing"*—taking each step in the sight of your *Abba*.

As our Father has watched the way that we walk, so should we watch the ways of the Father. May we readily seek His counsel and be quick to heed His voice, knowing that His love will always apprehend us— whether we listen to Him or not. Our Father's love is everlasting, and either in discipline or blessing, it will overtake us. Let us commit our feet to His path alone, knowing in full the faithfulness of a Father: *"ADONAI your God is with you…"*

෴ ෴

Father, You pick me up and carry me like a son; You are faithful to never let me down. I praise You, ADONAI, and heed the warning of Your word—give ear to me in troubled times, and hear my voice when I am in need. Teach me Your ways, O God, that I will never stray, but walk only according to Your way. By Your loving hand, Lord God—be it of comfort or correction—may I live only for You… and lack not one single thing…

Messianic Torah Devotional **143**

ואתחנן

And I Pleaded for Grace
דְּבָרִים D'variym (Deuteronomy) 3:23-7:11

*"Ask now about the former days which existed
before you, from the day that God shaped man on
the earth, and from one end of the heavens even to
the other end of the heavens, whether there has
been [such a] great thing as this—or has [anything]
been heard like it? Has a people heard the voice of
[a] god speaking out of the midst of the fire as you
have heard; you—and lived? Or has [a] god tried
to go in to take to Himself a nation from the midst
of another nation by trials, by signs, by wonders,
and by war, and by a strong hand... and by great
terrors like all that ADONAI your God has done for
you... before your eyes?"* דְּבָרִים *D'variym 4:32-34*

Matchless, unequaled, nothing like it whatsoever in
all of human history... not since God created man from
the dust of the ground had anyone in the heavens above
or on the earth beneath witnessed *"[such a] great thing
as this." "The voice of [a] god speaking"* to a people—
unheard of. A god *"[taking] to Himself a nation from
the midst of another nation"*—beyond compare. From
one end of heaven to the other, no one but the least of
all peoples was chosen to bear witness to the awesome,
unparalleled acts of ADONAI our God.

A tiny, insignificant people was shown the great
and powerful deeds of ADONAI so that the very birth
and existence of their nation would testify forever of His
sovereignty and might. The peculiar distinction of
Yis'rael from among all the nations of the earth granted
her a special audience with the King—a vantage point
shared by no other. *"For who is a greater nation that has
[a] god near to it"* (4:7) as ADONAI is near to you, O
Yis'rael? *"For you are a holy people to ADONAI your God.
In you has ADONAI your God chosen to be His own
treasured people out of all the peoples who are on the face
of the ground [of the earth]."* (7:6)

And yet—for all the awesome displays of power, for
all the nearness and chosenness of the people—if Yis'rael
does not testify to the spectacle of her salvation, it is all
for nothing. One way or another, the witness of Yis'rael
must go forth to the nations to proclaim the one, true
God—the God of Av'raham, Yitz'chak and Yis'rael. All
peoples of the earth need to know about the God who
speaks to men and lets them live—the God who faithfully
fights for the ones He loves, and separates them for
Himself. Let all creation ring with the testimony of
Yis'rael, for ADONAI is worthy to be praised. Indeed,
*"what god [is there] in the heavens or on earth who can do
deeds and mighty acts"* like our God? (3:24)

*"And because He loved your fathers, in their
seed after them He also chose, and brought you out
by His Presence—by His great power—from
מִצְרַיִם, Mitz'rayim: to dispossess nations greater
and stronger than you... to bring you in to give to
you their Land—an inheritance, as at this day.
And you will know today, and will turn it back to
your heart, that ADONAI, He is God, in the heavens
above, and on the earth beneath—there is none
else."* דְּבָרִים D'variym 4:37-39

"*Before [their] eyes,*" ADONAI demonstrated His supreme authority—His sovereign will was declared in the sight of all Yis'rael. But He wielded His power not solely out of mercy, nor just for the sake of a promise made long before. No, the end of the plan—which would eventually mean life for all the peoples—was for Yis'rael to "*know... and turn* it *back to [their] heart, that ADONAI, He is God,*" and there is no other.

"*Ask now about the former days... and from* one *end of the heavens*" to the other: what is the testimony that the world hears today from the lips of the people of Yis'rael? Who among this least of all nations cries out such that the lifeless gods of the world shudder and faint at the sound? Who declares the wonders of ADONAI, so that all creation may hear of His majesty?

May we turn our hearts toward the sons of Yis'rael, that *their* hearts may be turned back to ADONAI—and their mouths be opened to declare His Salvation. Let the mighty acts of God be seen once again among "*His own treasured people,*" that they might finally enter into the fullness of their inheritance. Let us declare to Yis'rael the "*Presence... [and] great power*" of their firstborn Son, so that they will know and testify before heaven and earth "*that ADONAI, He is God... there is none else.*"

৯৯ ৯৬

Who is like You, ADONAI, in the heavens above and on the earth beneath? No one, my God!—there is none else! Holy One of Yis'rael, turn back the hearts of Your chosen ones—restore Your own treasured people as a witness of Your strength and power. Make Your presence known to Your people, ADONAI, that their mouths may proclaim Your awesome deeds. By the testimony of Your sanctified ones, Lord, may all creation know its *Yeshua*. Truly, ADONAI, God of Yis'rael, there is *none* like You...

עקב

Because
דְּבָרִים D'variym (Deuteronomy) 7:12-11:25

"Do not speak in your heart… saying, '[It is]
because [of] my righteousness [that] ADONAI has
brought me in to possess this Land.' [Rather, it is]
for the wickedness of these nations [that] ADONAI
is dispossessing them…. Know that [it is] not for
your righteousness… for a people stiff of neck you
are. Remember—do not forget—that with which
you have made ADONAI your God angry in the
wilderness. Even from the day that you had come
out of the land of מִצְרַיִם, Mitz'rayim until your
coming in to this place, rebels you have been with
ADONAI." דְּבָרִים D'variym 9:4,6-7

After being told a half-dozen times that you're the
chosen people of God, it's conceivable that you might
develop a slightly inflated self-image. This, of course,
would be an understatement for the children of Yis'rael,
given their tendency to deem themselves upright when
in fact they have been stiff-necked, provocative rebels.
Surely Moshe's gentle and succinct reminder to the
contrary was greatly appreciated by all the people. After
all, who doesn't love reminiscing about that whole
molten calf debacle? Nothing like a nice, big slice of
humble *manna* to put things into perspective…

We deserve to be knocked down a few pegs when we think that we are the center of God's universe. We're not doing Him a favor when we go to Him in prayer, and He's not just sitting around waiting for us to call. Though we may like to believe that answers to prayer are custom-made just for us, we *might* simply be getting someone else's leftovers... we need to *"know that [it is] not for [our] righteousness"* that He blesses and cares for us.

"Remember—do not forget" that when He brings us in to possess the land, there's some poor fool about to the get the boot... who thinks he's just as great as you.

> *"Behold, to ADONAI your God belong the heavens and the heavens of the heavens, the earth and all that is in it. Yet in your fathers has ADONAI delighted—to love them, and He has chosen in their seed after them—in you—out of all the peoples as at this day. And you—circumcise the foreskin of your heart; and your neck—[do] not stiffen anymore. For ADONAI your God—He is God of the gods, and Master of the masters; God, the great, the mighty, and the fearful, who recognizes not faces [then shows partiality], nor takes a bribe.... He is your praise, and He is your God, who has done with you these great and fearful things which your eyes have seen."* דְּבָרִים *D'variym 10:14-17, 21*

Compared to the splendor of creation—the spectacular breadth of the heavens, the amazing wonders of the earth—we are but a speck... a minuscule, diminutive, infinitesimal dot. What good are we to the *"God of the gods, and Master of the masters"*—*"the great, the mighty"* One? ADONAI owns even *"the heavens of the heavens, the earth and all that is in it,"* and yet, His

delight is in the one thing in all creation that gives Him
any grief—marvelous, insignificant, stiff-of-neck... *us.*

For all the arrogance of unbent knees and unbowed
heads, for all the conceit of self-exaltation and withheld
praise, we remain the prize of ADONAI's divine collection.
It is in us that He finds pleasure—it is we whom He
loves and treasures. In the endless expanse of His
everlasting kingdom, there is no compare to the glory
and magnificence of man.

Under the weight of our worth, may we crumple in
humility before our Maker; may we bow down before
the One whose appraisal alone assigns us any value. Let
us *"circumcise the foreskin of [our] heart[s]; and [our]
neck[s]—stiffen not anymore,"* that we may yield
ourselves and submit our lives to the Creator of being
and breath. Let us see ourselves through the eyes of
ADONAI—no smaller, nor greater, than He has made us
to be. For *"He* is *your praise, and He* is *your God, who
has done with you these great and fearful things..."*

೪ ೪

Behold, ADONAI my God, to You alone belong the
heavens and the earth—You reign over every god and
master, for all creation is Yours alone. Humble me, O
God, that I will not think myself so significant and
righteous; though You exalt me over every created
thing, subdue my arrogance and pride. I bless You,
great and mighty One, who knows my face, yet shows
me no preference. I lose myself to You and bow to You
my will—my Master, my praise, and my God...

ראה

See
דְּבָרִים D'variym (Deuteronomy) 11:26-16:17

"When ADONAI your God cuts off the nations
(those which you are going in to dispossess) from
your presence, and you have dispossessed them and
have dwelled in their land, [and] after they have
been destroyed out of your presence, guard yourself,
lest you be ensnared [to] follow them, and lest you
inquire about their gods, saying, 'How do these
nations serve their gods that I [may] do so—even
I?' You must not do so to ADONAI your God; for
every abomination… which He hates, they have
done to their gods…." דְּבָרִים D'variym 12:29-31

ADONAI promised that He would "cut off" the nations
from the Land He was giving to His people. Yis'rael was
then to go in and "destroy out of [their] presence" every
shred of evidence of previous occupation. The high
places and sacred poles and altars dedicated to false
gods—these especially were to be smashed, burned, and
completely obliterated. But if there would be nothing
left so as to "ensnare" Yis'rael and tempt the people to
"inquire about [other] gods," why the cause for alarm?

The allure of the forbidden will make us go far out
of our way. If it means satisfying the hunger of infidelity,

we will actively evade the holy and seek the wicked and the abominable. Even the memory of the way things used to be is sufficient to draw us away, enticing us to pursue the phantoms of an ungodly past. It's not enough, then, to merely rid ourselves of the people and objects that lead us astray. Instead, we must be on guard in our *hearts* and remain faithful to what is pure... never quenching the thirst for what we've been told we cannot have.

> *"...you must purge the evil from your midst. When your brother, [a] son of your mother, or your son, or your daughter, or the wife you cherish, or your friend who is as your own soul entices you in secret, saying, 'Let us go and serve other gods,' (which you have not known, you and your fathers, of the gods of the peoples who are round about you, who are near to you, or who are far off from you, from the [one] end of the earth even to the [other] end of the earth), do not consent to him, nor listen to him, nor may your eye have pity on him, nor will you spare nor... hide him. But you must surely kill him; your hand will be on him [first]... to put him to death, and the hand of all the people last. And you will stone him with stones, and he will die, for he has sought to drive you away from ADONAI your God.... And all יִשְׂרָאֵל, Yis'rael will hear [of it] and fear, and [try] to do like this evil word in your midst no more."* דְּבָרִים *D'variym 13:5(6)-11(12)*

The utterance of unfaithfulness searches relentlessly for an eager ear—and it will exploit even the channels of intimacy to find one. Though we may zealously guard ourselves against external enticements, we remain vulnerable to trusted voices that might whisper of betrayal. Against the vigilant, there is but one way to effectively transmit the disease: the virus of adultery can only be carried in the mouth of the one we trust and love.

With nothing but a kiss, we contract the fatal illness; the poison instantly surges through our veins. We reel backward in complete dismay—horrified and stunned by our sudden contamination. The reality of our condition swiftly sets in, and we know there is only one hope for survival. The treatment is extreme; the consequences severe... *"you must purge the evil from your midst."*

We must never *"consent... [or] listen to"* the voice of a stranger who seeks *"to drive [us] away from ADONAI [our] God,"* but we must also be prepared to silence even the secret inducements of those whom we treasure and adore. As much as we love *"the wife [we] cherish, or [the] friend who* is *as [our very] own soul,"* nothing is permitted to come between us and our God—and the *"evil word"* can exist *"in [our] midst no more."*

ào ∽

ADONAI my God, destroy me from out of Your presence should I ever seek to follow after other gods. May I hunger and thirst only for You, O Lord, and be abundantly satisfied by the provision of Your unending faithfulness. Teach me Your jealousy, O God, and show me the breadth of Your zeal, that I may fear the consequences of infidelity and be ruthless for the sake of Your Name. I bless You, ADONAI, the Mighty God, You who are above all others—for from one end of the earth even to the other, there is no one I love like You.

שפטים

Judges

דְּבָרִים **D'variym (Deuteronomy) 16:18-21:9**

"For these nations who you are dispossessing:
to observers of clouds and to diviners do [they]
listen. But you—not so has ADONAI your God
permitted you. A prophet like me [Moshe], out
of your midst, out of your brothers, will ADONAI
your God raise up for you—to him you [must]
listen. [This is] according to all that you asked of
ADONAI your God in חֹרֵב, Chorev, in the day of
the assembly [when you] said, 'Let me not again
hear the voice of ADONAI my God, and of this
great fire let me not see anymore, and I [will]
not die.'" דְּבָרִים D'variym 18:14-16

We stood trembling at the foot of the mountain.
We saw the billowing smoke; we felt the heat of the fire;
we heard the roar of growing thunder. As lightning
pierced the sky, the sound of the *shofar* trumpeted the
descent of ADONAI—from the heavens He came down
to declare His word in the midst of the assembly. Out
of His own mouth, our God announced to us the
breadth of the commands that would keep us as a
people. ADONAI spoke to us and gave to us His Torah...

...and we asked for Messiah!

When we openly heard the voice of the Lord, we begged Moshe not to let us hear it again. We said it would be sufficient for *Moshe* to speak to us—to hear God's voice through him instead. By asking for a prophet, we spoke well, and ADONAI was pleased with our response. Yet the prophet would not be Moshe our Deliverer, but rather *"a prophet like [him]"* whom God Himself would one day *"raise up."*

While the nations search in futility for answers, attempting to divine mysteries from the clouds, ADONAI speaks clearly to us through His Prophet, the Messiah Yeshua—and it is *"to him [alone that we are permitted to] listen."* In His mouth and in His being is the Word of ADONAI, and to all that He says and is, we must reply. *"For the Torah through Moshe was given; the grace and the truth through Yeshua HaMashiyach did come."* *(Yn.1:17)* The One that He promised has been *"raise[d] up"*… will we now do all that He says, and live?

> *"And ADONAI said to me, 'They have done well that they have spoken. A prophet I [will] raise up to them, out of the midst of their brothers, like to you [Moshe]. And I will put my words in his mouth, and he will speak to them all that which I command him. And it will be—the man who does not listen to My words which he will speak in My Name, I [will nevertheless] require it of him.'"* דְּבָרִים *D'variym 18:17-19*

The fearsome and deafening noise shook us to the core, so we cowered and covered our heads at the awesome voice of the Lord. Now, the muffled cries of the Master Yeshua go out for all to hear—He is calling Yis'rael to listen to Him speak God's word… to once and for all unstop her willful, self-shut ears.

We asked for a way to understand the Torah of
ADONAI without having to listen to His voice—and yet
we turn a deaf ear to the mouth ADONAI chose to tell us
the very words we long to hear. *Mashiyach* is speaking
with longing to us—"*all that which [ADONAI] command[s]
him*" is on His lips. We can refuse to listen as long as
we like, and continue to wait for someone else to come,
but we will nevertheless be required to give an account
of why we ignored the voice of God's Only Son.

The Messiah of Yis'rael came to us not merely by
ADONAI's sovereign will—He was raised up to become
our Salvation because *we* asked for Him to be sent! Did
He simply show up unannounced? Had we not been
told to expect Him? Indeed, it was we who extended
the invitation in the first place, though we now fail to
acknowledge that He has arrived.

We heard the voice of God, but couldn't handle the
sound, so we pleaded for another to speak on His
behalf. Now ADONAI our God has given us the Messiah
that we asked for—isn't it about time that we listened to
what He's been dying to say?

❧ ❧

Messiah of Yis'rael, Master Yeshua, Living and
Spoken Word of God—speak to me now, declare Your
Torah... I am listening to all You have been commanded
to say. May Your people Yis'rael see Your glory, my
King, the people whose mouths begged for Your
intercession. Open our ears that we may hear of Your
Salvation and reply with words of profession and sounds
of praise. I bless You, ADONAI my God, for Your word
is not hidden in the heavens—from the lips of Your
Prophet, it is made clearly known. I worship You,
Redeemer and Deliverer of all—tell me everything You
have been waiting for me to finally know...

כי תצא

When You Go
דְּבָרִים D'variym (Deuteronomy) 21:10-25:19

"A place you [must] have at the outside of the camp, and you will 'go' there outside, and a peg you [will] have on your staff, and it will be, when you sit outside, that you will dig [a hole] with it, then turn back [the ground] and cover your excrement. For ADONAI your God walks up and down in the midst of your camp, to deliver you, and to give your enemies to you. And your camp must be holy, and He must not see in you the [indecent] nakedness of anything, or [He] will turn back away from you." דְּבָרִים *D'variym 23:12(13)-14(15)*

When you're the author of a devotional book about the Torah, and you come to the portion regarding cross-dressing, promiscuity, rape, emasculation, and prostitution; naturally, you gravitate toward the verses concerning proper bathroom etiquette. Now, given such a colorful subject, you have to be careful not to cross the line that separates clever from crude. But this is the Torah of ADONAI—surely we'll find someplace to go with this line of thinking.

Many of us tend to flush at the idea of openly discussing an issue as personal as waste elimination, but just because something makes us uncomfortable, that doesn't mean we have permission to avoid it. Moshe had a very good reason to instruct the people about where and how to relieve themselves: "ADONAI your God walks up and down in the midst of your camp." Telling the Lord to watch His step… well now, that just wouldn't do.

We may not want to talk about it, but that doesn't change the fact that we all know how to stink up a place. Though it's part of our nature and everyone does it, it's wrong to make a great big mess and then leave it sitting around to defile everyone else. In Messiah, "your camp must be holy," and we have to take responsibility for cleaning up the messes that we make. Let's not wallow in "the [indecent] nakedness of anything," but rather go outside the camp and dig that hole… burying our business where it belongs.

> "And if a man['s brother dies, and he] does
> not delight to take his brother's wife… then have
> [her] draw near to him before the eyes of the elders,
> and remove his shoe from off his foot, and spit in
> his face, and testify and say, 'Thus it is done to the
> man who will not build up the house of his brother!
> And his name will be called in יִשְׂרָאֵל, Yis'rael,
> "The House of Him Whose Shoe is Removed."'"
> דְּבָרִים D'variym 25:7-10

It's bad enough stepping in someone else's stuff—but it's much worse doing it barefoot. Why else would the prospect of having our shoes removed be a deterrent against failing to fulfill our obligations?

In what might appear to us as a bizarre—even silly—ritual, a widow confronts her brother-in-law when he refuses to *"build up the house of his brother."* Apparently, she takes off only *one* of his shoes, spits in his face, and then publicly ridicules him by calling him names. Now, while some of us may secretly fantasize about doing likewise to someone we know, it seems somewhat immature and futile—especially since you can't take the *other* shoe, too. Why, then, is this the sanctioned solution for a woman so thoughtlessly wronged?

When we neglect our duty, we *should* lose our loafers, making it harder to walk our own way. If we're going to hurt someone by failing to live up to our responsibilities, we should suffer as well, treading unshod along the sullied path of abandonment. Let us instead travel the road toward fulfilled obligation with clad feet, dried eyes, and unscathed reputations. May our toes know the security of being insulated in righteousness, as our sense of duty and honor fills us up all the way from the depths of our *soles.*

&> <&

God of Yis'rael, Creator of all things, no subject is too crude if it will draw me closer to You. Lord God, I loathe the mess I make when I am not walking in the holiness of Your word—teach me Your ways, ADONAI, that I will always know when and which way to go. I praise You, Lord, for You would rather remove my shoe than allow me to walk comfortably in my rebellious ways. Guide me, O God, back to the path of Your word, to which I am forever obliged to honor and obey. I bless You, ADONAI my God—may You never *"turn [Your] back away."* Make me holy, Lord, my encampment clean, that You may walk freely in me...

כי תבוא

When You Come In
דְּבָרִים **D'variym (Deuteronomy) 26:1-29:9(8)**

*"And it will be, if you will listen diligently to
the voice of ADONAI your God, to guard [and] to
do all His commands which I am commanding
you today, that ADONAI your God will make you
highest above all the nations of the earth, and all
these blessings will come upon you, and overtake
you, because you have listened to the voice of
ADONAI your God.... ADONAI [will] give [you]
your enemies... in one way they [will] come out to
you, and in seven ways before you they [will] flee....
And ADONAI will make you as [the] head, and not
as [the] tail, and you will be only [on] top, and will
not be [on the] bottom, for you will listen to the
commands of ADONAI your God... to guard and to
do [them]...."* דְּבָרִים *D'variym 28:1-2, 7, 13*

You won't be able to run fast enough; they will hunt
you relentlessly and never give up. You will feel them
gaining on you—closing in... soon, it will all be over. As
you finally succumb to the inevitable, you begin to sense
the enveloping presence of your pursuers. The last thing
you know as you are suddenly apprehended is the sound
of your own cries... for joy. You have been overcome
and overtaken by the abundance of ADONAI's blessings.

We will be unable to stop the outpouring upon us, *"if [we] will listen diligently to the voice of* Adonai *[our] God."* When we guard and do His word, obeying the commands of our Master, we will find ourselves drowning in the riches of a life free from fear—an existence overflowing with inescapable happiness.

Adonai rejoices to sweep us away in a downpour of His unending love. Nothing can stand against our God when He sets His will to empty heaven on our heads. Our submissive response to a simple *"if"* will yield showers of peace and prosperity greater than we can bear. May we take pleasure in pleasing Adonai our God, and surrender to the blessings that will soon hold us in their hands.

"And it will be, if you will not listen to the voice of Adonai *your God to guard [and] to do all His commands and His statutes which I command you today—that all these curses will come upon you, and overtake you.... * Adonai *[will] give you defeat before your enemies; in one way you [will] go out to them, and in seven ways before them [you] will flee.... The sojourner who is in your midst [will] be very high above you... he will be as [the] head, and you will be as [the] tail... Because you did not listen to the voice of* Adonai *your God... it will be, [that] as* Adonai *has rejoiced over you to do you good... so will* Adonai *rejoice over you to destroy you... and* Adonai *will scatter you among the peoples, from one end of the earth even to the [other]...."* דְּבָרִים *D'variym 28:15, 25, 43-44, 62-64*

We won't be able to run fast enough; they will hunt us relentlessly and never give up. We will sense them gaining on us—closing in... soon, it will all be over. As we finally succumb to the inevitable, we begin to feel the enveloping presence of our pursuers. The last thing we know as we are suddenly apprehended is the sound of our own cries... in terror. We have been overcome and overtaken by the horde of the curses of ADONAI.

We will be unable to stop the torrent against us, *"if [we] will not listen to the voice of ADONAI [our] God."* When we abandon and ignore His covenant, disobeying the commands of our Master, we will find ourselves drowning in the flood of a life consumed with fear—an existence overrun with inescapable destruction. ADONAI rejoices to sweep us away in a deluge of His unending rage. Nothing can stand against our God when He sets His will to empty His wrath on our heads.

Our rebellious response to a simple *"if"* will yield a downpour of confusion and loss greater than we can bear. Should we not, then, answer His *"if"* with our "yes," and forego His curses for blessing? Let us *"listen to the voice of ADONAI our God,"* and hear the promises He is swearing before us today... because no matter which reward we choose—the blessing or the curse—we *will* be overtaken.

৯০ ৬৯

ADONAI my God, chase me and run me down; heap Your blessings upon me, Lord, and bury me. In all my ways, O God, prosper me with life, as I remain joyfully obedient to You. Do not let me wander from You, ADONAI, but catch me with Your judgment should I stray. May all my running from You be in vain, my Master—overcome me with the full weight of my reward. I give You praise and honor, glorious One, who withholds nothing from those whom He loves. Whether by the blessing or the curse, O God of Yis'rael, overtake me and never let me go...

Nitzaviym

נצבים

Standing
דְּבָרִים D'variym (Deuteronomy) 29:10(9)-30:20

*"For this command which I am commanding
you today, it is not too extraordinary for you, nor
is it far off. It is not in the heavens [that you should
be] saying, 'Who will go up for us into the heavens
and will get it for us, and will cause us to hear it,
that we may do it?' And it is not beyond the sea
[that you should be] saying, 'Who will pass over
for us beyond the sea, and will get it for us, and will
cause us to hear it, that we may do it?' For very
near to you is the Word—in your mouth, and in
your heart—to do it."* דְּבָרִים *D'variym 30:11-14*

Impossible: that's how we see it. It's completely out
of our reach—there's no way we can do it. Hasn't the
Lord placed unrealistic expectations on us? After all,
we're only human—we shouldn't be required to do
everything He says. If ADONAI *really* loves us, then He'll
just cover us with His grace. We only need to *love* the
Lord... what more could He reasonably expect us to do?

The Word of ADONAI is *"not too extraordinary"* for
us, *"nor* is *it far off"* and out of our reach. To suggest
otherwise is to call God a liar, and ignore the very Word
we are exhorted to hear. *"It is not in the heavens,"* nor

"beyond the sea"—we don't need someone to go get it
for us and tell us what it means. ADONAI's Word is not
so distant and lofty after all, *"for very near to you is the
Word—in your mouth, and in your heart..."* and He has
every reason to expect we can *"do it."*

> *"See, I have set before you today life and good,
> and death and evil, in that I am commanding you
> today to love ADONAI your God, to walk in His
> ways, to keep His commands, and His statutes, and
> His judgments; and you will live and increase, and
> ADONAI your God will bless you in the land where
> you are going in to possess it.... I have caused to
> testify against you today the heavens and the earth.
> Life and death I have set before you; the blessing
> and the cursing. And [now] choose life, so that you
> will live, you and your seed, to love ADONAI your
> God, to listen to His voice, and to cling to Him—
> for He is your life, and the length of your days...."*
> דְּבָרִים *D'variym 30:15-16,19-20*

Within the Word we find our fate—and it is greatly
lacking in shades of gray. Life or death; good or evil;
the blessing and the cursing—our options are severely
limited. Most of us don't like such black and white
terms, and so rather than choosing, we spend our lives
testing out alternatives. But there are no secret paths
that will lead us to the love of God. We either *"walk in
His ways,"* or we're walking away. The choice between
extremes appears a simple one—*"life"* seems to be the
obvious choice. But when we *"choose life,"* whose life
are we choosing? Are we prepared for the *death* it
entails?

If we *"choose life,"* will we *"listen to His voice,"*
heeding His Word and turning a deaf ear to our own?

If we *"choose life,"* will we *"cling to Him"* with all our strength, taking hold of *Him* as we let *ourselves* go? By choosing to live, we are obligating ourselves to a life that no longer belongs to us. When we *"choose life,"* then *"He [becomes our] life,"* and the life we now have is no more.

Life versus death, good versus evil—our God versus ourselves. These are the plain and simple choices set before us… and yet here we are, still trying to make up our minds. If we truly *"love ADONAI [our] God,"* we will do more than just give Him our hearts. We will do as He says, give Him our ears and our hands, and gain life through the loss of ourselves.

"Life and death I have set before you; the blessing and the cursing." Make your decision wisely and soon… as if your life depends on it.

෯෯ ෯෯

ADONAI my God, may heaven and earth testify against me this day—I love You and I will listen only to *Your* voice… I choose life! Thank You, O God, for not hanging Your Word so high above me that I cannot reach it. Instead, You have planted it in my heart and placed it on my lips, that I can do it—and by it, I will live. Teach me, ADONAI, to walk in Your ways, and to cling to You alone for my very life. Let all creation hear the declaration I make today: I am no longer; You are the life that I live….

Vayelech

וילך

And He Went
דְּבָרִים D'variym (Deuteronomy) 31:1-30

"ADONAI your God—He will pass over before you, He will destroy these nations from before you, and you will possess them.... And ADONAI will give them [over] before your face, and you will do to them according to all the commands which I have commanded you. Be strong and courageous, fear not, nor be terrified because of them, for ADONAI your God is He who is going with you. He will not fail nor leave you." דְּבָרִים *D'variym 31:3,5-6*

The sons of Yis'rael would soon suffer the loss of the first and only leader they had ever known. Shortly thereafter, they would embark upon the campaign of destiny that would forever define their existence as a nation. To an entire generation, ADONAI had proven Himself faithful—time and again, He displayed His power and strength in their sight. Now, face to face with the future they had been waiting for, Yis'rael was prepared to surge forward in faith and victory. Moshe stood before them in his final address to encourage and exhort the people of Yis'rael. *"He will pass over before you, He will destroy these nations from before you,"* you will have complete and total success, *"for ADONAI your God is He who is going with you."*

"*Be strong and courageous, fear not, nor be terrified*"—
this was the message Moshe proclaimed that day. By
doing "*according to all the commands which I have
commanded you,*" Yis'rael was assured a triumph over
all her enemies. When we walk confidently and
obediently in the steps of ADONAI, we too have this
assurance. By holding fast to His word, "*ADONAI [our]
God... [goes] with [us],*" and "*He will not fail [us] nor
leave...*"

> "*And ADONAI said to* מֹשֶׁה, *Moshe, 'Behold,
> you will lie down with your fathers, and this people
> will rise [up] and go commit adultery with the
> gods of the foreigner... and [will] leave Me, and
> break My covenant which I made with them. So
> My anger will burn against them in that day, and I
> will leave them, and hide My face from them... for
> all the evil which they will do, for they will turn to
> other gods.... And [when] I bring them in onto the
> ground [of the Land] which I have sworn to their
> fathers—flowing with milk and honey—and they
> have eaten, and been satisfied, and become fat,
> [they] will turn to other gods, and they will serve
> them and despise Me, and break My covenant....
> For I know their [natural] predisposition....'*"
> דְּבָרִים *D'variym 31:16-18, 20-21*

Following Moshe's discourse of encouragement and
anticipation, ADONAI took him aside to give him the
deflating news. After forty long and tireless years of
intercession, teaching and preparation, the people of
Yis'rael will go in and possess the Land only to "*rise [up]
and go commit adultery with the gods of the foreigner.*"
The covenant will be shattered; they will turn their
backs on the God who loves them. Without shame,

they will flaunt their fornication, forcing ADONAI to do the one thing He said He would never do: leave.

Is this not the fate we all face if we turn away from ADONAI our God? Though He cares for us and loves us and raises us as His children, *"[He] will leave [us], and hide [His] face from [us]… for all the evil which [we] will do."* ADONAI pours out His blessings upon us, providing abundantly for our every need. So when we *"have eaten"* from His hand *"and been satisfied,"* let us not *"become fat"* and despise the One who nourishes us.

May we be a "surprise" to ADONAI our God and walk not according to our *"[natural] predisposition."* Instead, let us go in the way we have been instructed, guarding the integrity of the covenant that ADONAI keeps faithfully with us. Let us not *"commit adultery"* against our God, but commit our lives to serving Him— and Him alone. Then we will have full assurance that *"He will not fail nor leave [us],"* and for all our days we will always see His face.

⇛ ⇚

ADONAI my God, I willfully submit to Your awesome and humbling ways. Fill me with Your Spirit, Lord God of Yis'rael, that I may follow You alone and forsake the natural inclinations of my heart. I praise You, O God, for You not only show me the path, but You go on it before me in power. Draw me to You, my Master, and teach me to never stray, that I may walk with confidence in the promise that You will never leave. I give glory to Your Name, ADONAI—faithful and unfailing One. You deserve all honor and praise, great and mighty God— the Strength of all my days…

Give Ear
דְּבָרִים D'variym (Deuteronomy) 32:1-52

"And יְשֻׁרוּן, Y'shurun grows fat and kicks: you have been fat, you have been thick, you have been engorged. And he rejects God who made him, and dishonors the Rock of his salvation. They made Him jealous with strangers—with abominations they make Him angry. They sacrifice to demons—'non-god[s]'! Gods they have not known—new ones—from nearby they came; your fathers have not feared them! You forget the Rock that birthed you, and neglect God who formed you." דְּבָרִים D'variym 32:15-18

Moshe sings a familiar tune, but Yis'rael won't play along. The title has changed, but not the verse or refrain; it's still just the same old song.

"You have been fat, you have been thick," you have feasted until *"engorged"*—upon the reward of ADONAI's provision you have dined. So now that you have eaten, you bite the hand that feeds you—your insatiable appetite lusts for fruit of a foreign kind. *"Y'shurun grows fat and kicks"* against the *"God who made him."* He indulges himself, ungrateful for his blessings, rejecting the God who knows him. *"You forget the Rock that*

birthed you," Ya'akov, *"the Rock of [your] salvation."*
Why do you feed your face, Y'shurun, yet empty yourself
of righteousness?

The warning issued to Yis'rael, which ultimately
went unheeded, testifies against *us* today—will *we* fare
any better? Do we do obeisance to *"non-god[s]"* who
are powerless to save, yet govern our lives? Do we
"sacrifice to demons," allowing them to possess us, and
then do the abominable bidding of our ravenous minds?
What barren, feeble forces hold sway over our hearts
while the God of our lives is neglected and dishonored?
What hunger and thirst drives us to the arms of a
stranger and away from the One who loves us best of all?

For absolutely nothing, he recklessly exchanged
everything he could ever want. Upright Yis'rael has
fallen down—Y'shurun is his name... what's yours?

> *"They have made Me jealous by 'non-god[s]'—*
> *they made Me angry by their vain [idolatry]. So I*
> *[will] make them jealous by [a] 'non-people'—by*
> *a foolish nation I [will] make them angry.... See*
> *now, that I—I am He, and there is no god with Me.*
> *I put to death, and I keep alive; I have wounded,*
> *and I heal; and there is not from [out of] My hand*
> *one [who can] deliver."* דְּבָרִים *D'variym 32:21,39*

A wisp of air; a puff of smoke; the trunk of a tree;
the face of a rock. Void and Vain sneer fiendishly in
amusement as Jealous becomes enraged and consumed.

Yis'rael has *"made Me jealous"*—at the feet of
Worthless, they cast their devotion. *"They made Me*
angry by their vain" and empty idols—Nothingness
devours their praise. They provoke me to envy by

worshipping what isn't real, and to *"non-god[s]"* offering adoration. *"So I [will] make them jealous by [loving a] 'non-people,'"* and showering my affection on *"a foolish nation."*

Though Yis'rael's loss means gain for the world, let no one dance on his grave. *"For if God did not spare the natural branches" (Ro.11:21),* who will escape in their adulterous ways? ADONAI expects a return on His love, which He gives without restraint or reserve. What good is such Love if it does not grow Jealous when nothing it receives is deserved?

"See now, that [He]... is He, and there is no god with [ADONAI]"—He is jealous for the love He is due. Do not be quick to exchange His affections for another, or He might trade someone else... for you.

೫ ೫

Lord God of Heaven and earth, may the song of my life be music to Your ears. I will sing of Your faithfulness and the abundance of Your love—how You pour out Your blessings, O Everlasting God. May I eat and be satisfied, hungering for no one but You, for You alone quench my thirst and fulfill my every desire. May I kick only against the wants of my flesh—in righteousness, may I always remember and fear my God. Spare me not, ADONAI, should I wander after nothing and despise the treasures of Your love. Have mercy, O Lord, in Your jealousy and anger, and draw me back to Your loving embrace once more. I give You all the honor and praise that is due Your glorious and wonderful Name. ADONAI my God, Husband and Father... You alone deserve my heart... and my life...

Vzot HaB'rachah

וזאת הברכה

And This Is the Blessing
דְּבָרִים D'variym (Deuteronomy) 33:1-34:12

"There is none like the God of יְשֻׁרוּן*, Y'shurun, riding the heavens to help you, and in His majesty the skies. A refuge is the eternal God, and beneath are [His] age-enduring arms. And he drives out from your presence the enemy, and says, 'Destroy!' And* יִשְׂרָאֵל*, Yis'rael dwells in confidence. Alone is the eye of* יַעֲקֹב*, Ya'akov in a land of grain and [new] wine. Also, His heavens drop down dew. O your happiness, O* יִשְׂרָאֵל*, Yis'rael! Who is like you? A people saved by* ADONAI*, the shield of your help, and He who is the sword of your majesty...."* דְּבָרִים *D'variym 33:26-29*

"There is none like [You]... God of Y'shurun"—You alone ride the skies in majesty. In the heavens above and on the earth beneath, You are matchless—Holy and Eternal God. You have loved and set apart Your people Yis'rael; You hold Your holy ones firmly in Your hand. You are worthy to be praised, for you keep Ya'akov, Your son... and yet, we do not recognize Your face.

Where is our *"help"* and our *"refuge,"* O God? Why are we strewn about the nations? Why do we not dwell in confident peace? Where is the joy of our salvation? *"A*

*people saved," yet lost we are—in the lands of strangers
we take shelter. We cannot find You—our Sword and
our Shield... where are Your "age-enduring arms"?*

Open our eyes, God of mercy and grace; unstop
our unhearing ears. Restore us as keepers of Your
covenant, My God, that Your Word we may always
hold near. A stubborn, rebellious, arrogant crew are
we, refusing the plain and simple truth. Humble us,
ADONAI, and let Your *"heavens drop down dew..."*

Hear O Yis'rael: *"Who is like you?"*

> *"And there has not arisen a prophet any more
> in לִשְׂרָאֵל, Yis'rael like מֹשֶׁה, Moshe whom ADONAI
> has known face to face in reference to all the signs
> and the wonders which ADONAI sent him to do in
> the land of מִצְרַיִם, Mitz'rayim to פַּרְעֹה, Par'oh
> and to all his servants and to all his land, and in
> reference to all [of] the [power of His] strong hand,
> and to all the great, awesome [deeds] which מֹשֶׁה,
> Moshe did before the eyes of יִשְׂרָאֵל, Yis'rael."*
> דְּבָרִים *D'variym 34:10-12*

From chains to freedom to the edge of inheritance,
Moshe did *"great, awesome [deeds]... before the eyes of
Yis'rael."* He was *"known face to face"* by the Creator of
all things, performing mighty *"signs and... wonders"* in
the midst of His people. When the length of his days had
drawn to a close, Moshe climbed one final mountain
and breathed his last. This may be the end of the Torah
of Moshe... but it is not yet the end of the tale.

"There has... arisen [another] prophet... in Yis'rael"
whom ADONAI also knows *"face to face."* He too has
done *"great [and] awesome... signs and... wonders"*—

"the eyes of Yis'rael" beheld His deeds of truth and grace. But unlike Moshe, He ascended not a mountain, but to His throne as Messiah and King. Like Moshe, He also took His last breath and expired—but with *new* life, *this* Prophet conquered death and the grave!

With veiled faces Yis'rael waits for a prophet who can take us only as far as the river—a man like Moshe who can give us the life of Torah, but not the power to live it. A Prophet like Moshe—yet greater than He— has written His Word on our souls. Sons of Yis'rael, behold! The Messiah Yeshua alone can lead us through the water… and bring us home!

❧ ❧

אֱלֹהֵי אַבְרָהָם אֱלֹהֵי יִצְחָק וֵאלֹהֵי יַעֲקֹב
אֲנִי מַאֲמִין כִּי יֵשׁוּעַ הַמָּשִׁיחַ בֶּן־הָאֱלֹהִים הוּא

'Elohei Av'raham, 'Elohei Yitz'chak,
velohei Ya'akov—'aniy ma'amiyn kiy
Yeshua HaMashiyach ben Ha'Elohiym hu!

God of Av'raham, Yitz'chak, and Ya'akov—I believe that Yeshua the Messiah is the Son of God! I give You everlasting glory and praise, my King, for You have removed the blindness and given light to my eyes. Thank You, O Lord, for softening my heart, that I may see and know You, My Redeemer. By *"[Your] strong hand,"* O God, You displayed Your awesome might and power—reviving me from the dead as a sign to all the peoples. My Sword and my Shield, call home Your sons, that we may proclaim the fullness of Your truth. My Savior and Master—Messiah, Yeshua—truly, there is none like You…

Glossary

This reverse glossary is alphabetized according to the transliterated English found throughout the devotionals. Each glossary entry includes the Hebrew, transliteration, and English translation or definition. Below is a pronunciation key to assist the reader with verbalization of the English transliterations.

Pronunciation Key			
a = "ah"	*e* = "eh"	*i* = "ee"	*o* = "oh"
u = "oo"	*ch* = guttural sound in back of throat, as in *"Bach"* or *"loch,"* not "ch" as in *"much"*		

אַבָּא	Abba	"Daddy"
אַחֲרֵי	ach'arei	after
יהוה	ADONAI	The "Sacred Name" of God, YHVH, represented by the substitution "Adonai" in all capital letters. (See Introduction for more information.)
אֲדֹנָי	Adonai	Lord, Master
אַהֲרוֹן	A'haron	Aaron
אָמֵן	amen	Truly, so be it
אֲנִי	aniy	"I"—first person pronoun
אָנֹכִי	anochiy	"I"—first person pronoun

אַבְרָהָם	Av'raham	Abraham
אַבְרָם	Av'ram	Abram
בָּלָק	Balak	Balak
בֵּית־אֵל	Beit-el	House of God
בְּחֻקֹּתַי	b'chukotai	"in my statutes"
בְּהַעֲלֹתְךָ	b'ha'alot'cha	"in your causing to go up"
בְּהַר	b'har	"on mount"
בִּלְעָם	Bil'am	Balaam
בִּן	bin	"son (of);" form of בֵּן, *ben*
בְּמִדְבַּר	b'mid'bar	"in the wilderness;" fifth word of the book of Numbers
בֹּא	bo	go, come
בְּרֵאשִׁית	b'reshiyt	"in the beginning;" first word of the book of Genesis
בְּרִית	b'riyt	covenant
בְּרִיתִי	b'riytiy	"my covenant (of)"
בְּשַׁלַּח	b'shalach	"when he let go"
חָרְמָה	Char'mah	Hormah
חַיֵּי שָׂרָה	Chayei Sarah	"Sarah's life"
חֹרֵב	Chorev	Horeb
חֻקַּת	chukat	statute
כֹּהֲנִים	co'haniym	plural for *cohen*
כֹּהֵן	cohen	priest
דְּבָרִים	d'variym	"words;" the second word in the book of Deuteronomy
עֵקֶב	ekev	because
אֵל	El	God
אֶלְעָזָר	El'azar	Eleazar
אֱלֹהֵי	'Elohei	"God of"
אֱלֹהִים	'Elohiym	God; literally "gods"

אֱמֹר	'emor	speak
אֱמֹרִי	'Emoriy	Amorites
עֵשָׂו	Esav	Esau
אֶרֶץ	eretz	land (of)
גָּד	Gad	Gad
גָּדִי	Gadiy	Gadites
גֹּשֶׁן	Goshen	Goshen
הַ	ha	"the," when it precedes another word
הָאָרֹן	HaAron	"The Ark" of the covenant
הַאֲזִינוּ	ha'aziynu	"give ear"
הַבְּרָכָה	HaB'rachah	"The Blessing"
הַכֹּהֵן	HaCohen	"The Priest"
הָאֵפֹד	HaEfod	"The Ephod;" priestly garment
הָאֵל	HaEl	literally, "The God"
הַגָּדֹל	HaGadol	"The High" (literally, "The Big" or "The Great"); as in, "The High Priest"
הַלְלוּ־יָהּ	Hal'lu-Yah	Hallelujah
הַמִּשְׁכָּן	HaMish'kan	"The Tabernacle"
הַיֹּבֵל	HaYovel	"The Jubilee"
כָּלֵב	Kalev	Caleb
כַּפֹּרֶת	kaporet	the ark cover; "mercy seat;" the place of atonement
קַיִן	Kayin	Cain
קְדֹשִׁים	k'doshiym	holy ones
כִּי	kiy	when (that, for, because)
כְּנַעַן	K'na-an	Canaan
קֹרַח	Korach	Korah
כְּרֻבִים	k'ruviym	cherubim
לֶךְ־לְךָ	lech-l'cha	"get yourself away"

לֵוִי	Leviy	Levite
לְוִיִּם	Leviyim	plural for *Leviy*
מָשִׁיחַ	Mashiyach	Messiah, meaning, "anointed one." In Greek, Χριστός, *Christos* (Christ)
מַסְעֵי	mas'ei	journeys
מַטּוֹת	matot	tribes
מִדְיָן	Mid'yan	Midian
מִקֵּץ	miketz	"at the end"
מִשְׁכָּן	mish'kan	tabernacle
מִשְׁכָּנִי	Mish'kaniy	"My Tabernacle"
מִשְׁפָּטִים	mish'patiym	judgments
מִצְרַיִם	Mitz'rayim	Egypt, Egyptians
מִצְרִי	Mitz'riy	Egyptian
מוֹאָב	Moav	Moab
מוֹאָבִי	Moaviy	Moabite
מֹשֶׁה	Moshe	Moses
מוֹת	mot	death
מְצֹרָע	m'tzora	"one being diseased"
נָשֹׂא	naso	"take up"
נִצָּבִים	nitzaviym	standing
נֹחַ	Noach	Noah
נוּן	Nun	Nun (father of Joshua)
פַּרְעֹה	Par'oh	Pharaoh
פִּינְחָס	Piyn'chas	Phinehas
פְּקוּדֵי	p'kudei	numberings
פְּנוּאֵל	P'nuel	Penuel
רְאֵה	r'eh	"see;" form of רָאָה, *ra-ah*
רִבְקָה	Riv'kah	Rebecca
רוּחַ	ruach	spirit
רְאוּבֵן	R'uven	Reuben
רְאוּבֵנִי	R'uveniy	Reubenites
שָׂרָה	Sarah	Sarah

שֵׂעִיר	Seiyr	Seir
שַׁבָּת	Shabbat	Sabbath
שַׁדַּי	Shadai	Almighty
שָׁלוֹם	shalom	peace, completeness
שִׁילֹה	Shiyloh	Shiloh
שְׁלַח־לְךָ	sh'lach-l'cha	"send for yourself"
שְׁמִינִי	sh'miyniy	"eighth"
שְׁמוֹת	sh'mot	"names"—second word of the book of Exodus
שְׁנַת	sh'nat	year (of); form of שָׁנָה, shanah
שׁוֹפָר	shofar	ram's horn
שֹׁפְטִים	shof'tiym	judges
שְׁאוֹל	Sh'ol	Sheol, the underworld
תָּבוֹא	tavo	come (in)
תַזְרִיעַ	taz'riya	"she gives seed"
תֵצֵא	tetze	go (out)
תִשָּׂא	tisa	take; take up
תּוֹדָה	todah	thanks; thank offering
תּוֹלְדֹת	tol'dot	genealogies
תּוֹרָה	Torah	Instruction, teaching, referring to the five books of Moses. Translated incorrectly as "Law."
תְּרוּמָה	t'rumah	offering
תְּצַוֶּה	t'tzaveh	"you are to command"
צָרַעַת	tzara-at	a skin disease; commonly "leprosy"
צַו	tzav	command
ו	vav	sixth letter of the Hebrew alef-beit; "and" when used as a prefix
וָאֵרָא	vaera	"and I appeared"

וָאֶתְחַנַּן	vaet'chanan	"and I pleaded for grace"
וַיַּקְהֵל	vayak'hel	"and (he) assembled"
וַיְחִי	vay'chiy	"and he lived"
וַיֵּלֶךְ	vayelech	"and he went"
וַיֵּרָא	vayera	"and he appeared"
וַיֵּשֶׁב	vayeshev	"and he dwelled"
וַיֵּצֵא	vayetze	"and he went out"
וַיִּגַּשׁ	vayigash	"and he came near"
וַיִּקְרָא	vayik'ra	"and (he) called"—first word of book of Leviticus
וַיִּשְׁלַח	vayish'lach	"and he sent"
וְזֹאת	v'zot	"and this"
יַעֲקֹב	Ya'akov	Jacob, James
יָהּ	Yah	Jah; shortened form of the "Sacred Name"
יַרְדֵּן	Yar'den	Jordan
יֵשׁוּעַ	Yeshua	salvation
יְהוֹשֻׁעַ	Y'hoshua	Joshua; "Yah saves"
יְהוּדָה	Y'hudah	Judah
יִשְׂרְאֵלִי	Yis'r'eliy	Israeli/Israelite
יִשְׂרְאֵלִים	Yis'r'eliym	Israelis/Israelites
יִשְׂרָאֵל	Yis'rael	Israel
יִתְרוֹ	Yit'ro	Jethro
יִצְחָק	Yitz'chak	Isaac
יוֹסֵף	Yosef	Joseph
יְשֻׁרוּן	Y'shurun	Jeshurun

APPENDIX A

The Torah Portions

Judaism's annual Torah reading cycle[1] is of unknown origin, though it is thought to have evolved from the early synagogue—perhaps even from before the time of Yeshua. The five books of Moses—Genesis through Deuteronomy—are divided into 54 portions, each one named for a key word or phrase at or very near the beginning of the portion. Each portion is further divided into seven *aliyot* to facilitate reading during the synagogue service. The final portion is to be read on the traditional Jewish holiday *Simchat Torah*, with the cycle beginning anew on the following Shabbat. With the exception of certain times that are allotted for special holiday readings, one Torah portion is traditionally read or studied each week.

The following five-year calendar[2] has been supplied for your convenience, should you choose to follow the traditional reading schedule for your Torah devotionals. While the traditional schedule only lists dates for synagogue readings on Shabbat, we have given you a *range* of dates for each portion, ending with the date from the traditional schedule. Since the length of Israel's calendar differs each year, during shorter years, certain Torah portions are grouped together. These "double portions" are indicated on the chart with brackets.

---

[1] There is a triennial (three-year) cycle as well.
[2] Traditional reading schedules for future years, as well as an alternate annual reading plan, are available on our website.

Portion	2008 / 2009	2009 / 2010
1. *B'reshiyt*	October 23-25	October 12-17
2. *Noach*	Oct. 26-Nov. 1	October 18-24
3. *Lech-L'cha*	November 2-8	October 25-31
4. *Vayera*	November 9-15	November 1-7
5. *Chayei Sarah*	November 16-22	November 8-14
6. *Tol'dot*	November 23-29	November 15-21
7. *Vayetze*	Nov. 30-Dec. 6	November 22-28
8. *Vayish'lach*	December 7-13	Nov. 29-Dec. 5
9. *Vayeshev*	December 14-20	December 6-12
10. *Miketz*	December 21-27	December 13-19
11. *Vayigash*	Dec. 28-Jan. 3	December 20-26
12. *Vay'chiy*	January 4-10	Dec. 27-Jan. 2
13. *Sh'mot*	January 11-17	January 3-9
14. *Vaera*	January 18-24	January 10-16
15. *Bo*	January 25-31	January 17-23
16. *B'shalach*	February 1-7	January 24-30
17. *Yit'ro*	February 8-14	Jan. 31-Feb. 6
18. *Mish'patiym*	February 15-21	February 7-13
19. *T'rumah*	February 22-28	February 14-20
20. *T'tzaveh*	March 1-7	February 21-27
21. *Kiy Tisa*	March 8-14	Feb. 28-March 6
22. *Vayak'hel*	} March 15-21	} March 7-13
23. *P'kudei*		
24. *Vayik'ra*	March 22-28	March 14-20
25. *Tzav*	Mar. 29-Apr. 4	March 21-27
26. *Sh'miyniy*	April 5-18	March 28-Apr. 10
27. *Taz'riya*	} April 19-25	} April 11-17
28. *M'tzora*		

continued on top of page 184

2010 / 2011	2011 / 2012	2012 / 2013
October 2	October 22	October 10-13
October 3-9	October 23-29	October 14-20
October 10-16	Oct. 30-Nov. 5	October 21-27
October 17-23	November 6-12	Oct. 28-Nov. 3
October 24-30	November 13-19	November 4-10
Oct. 31-Nov. 6	November 20-26	November 11-17
November 7-13	Nov. 27-Dec. 3	November 18-24
November 14-20	December 4-10	Nov. 25-Dec. 1
November 21-27	December 11-17	December 2-8
Nov. 28-Dec. 4	December 18-24	December 9-15
December 5-11	December 25-31	December 16-22
December 12-18	January 1-7	December 23-29
December 19-25	January 8-14	Dec. 30-Jan. 5
Dec. 26-Jan. 1	January 15-21	January 6-12
January 2-8	January 22-28	January 13-19
January 9-15	Jan. 29-Feb. 4	January 20-26
January 16-22	February 5-11	Jan. 27-Feb. 2
January 23-29	February 12-18	February 3-9
Jan. 30-Feb. 5	February 19-25	February 10-16
February 6-12	Feb. 26-March 3	February 17-23
February 13-19	March 4-10	Feb. 24-March 2
February 20-26 Feb. 27-March 5	} March 11-17	} March 3-9
March 6-12	March 18-24	March 10-16
March 13-19	March 25-31	March 17-23
March 20-26	April 1-21	March 24-Apr. 6
March 27-Apr. 2 April 3-9	} April 22-28	} April 7-13

continued on top of page 185

(continued)	2009	2010
29. *Ach'arei Mot*	} April 26-May 2	} April 18-24
30. *K'doshiym*		
31. *'Emor*	May 3-9	April 25-May 1
32. *B'har*	} May 10-16	} May 2-8
33. *B'chukotai*		
34. *B'mid'bar*	May 17-23	May 9-15
35. *Naso*	May 24-June 6	May 16-22
36. *B'ha'alot'cha*	June 7-13	May 23-29
37. *Sh'lach-L'cha*	June 14-20	May 30-June 5
38. *Korach*	June 21-27	June 6-12
39. *Chukat*	} June 28-July 4	June 13-19
40. *Balak*		June 20-26
41. *Piyn'chas*	July 5-11	June 27-July 3
42. *Matot*	} July 12-18	} July 4-10
43. *Mas'ei*		
44. *D'variym*	July 19-25	July 11-17
45. *Vaet'chanan*	July 26-Aug. 1	July 18-24
46. *Ekev*	August 2-8	July 25-31
47. *R'eh*	August 9-15	August 1-7
48. *Shof'tiym*	August 16-22	August 8-14
49. *Kiy Tetze*	August 23-29	August 15-21
50. *Kiy Tavo*	Aug. 30-Sep. 5	August 22-28
51. *Nitzaviym*	} September 6-12	} Aug. 29-Sep. 4
52. *Vayelech*		
53. *Ha'aziynu*	September 13-26	September 5-11
54. *V'zot HaB'rachah*	Sep. 27-Oct. 11	Sep. 12-Oct. 1

2011	2012	2013
April 10-16 April 17-30	} April 29-May 5	} April 14-20
May 1-7	May 6-12	April 21-27
May 8-14 May 15-21	} May 13-19	} April 28-May 4
May 22-28	May 20-26	May 5-11
May 29-June 4	May 27-June 2	May 12-18
June 5-11	June 3-9	May 19-25
June 12-18	June 10-16	May 26-June 1
June 19-25	June 17-23	June 2-8
June 26-July 2	June 24-30	June 9-15
July 3-9	July 1-7	June 16-22
July 10-16	July 8-14	June 23-29
July 17-23 July 24-30	} July 15-21	} June 30-July 6
July 31-August 6	July 22-28	July 7-13
August 7-13	July 29-August 4	July 14-20
August 14-20	August 5-11	July 21-27
August 21-27	August 12-18	July 28-August 3
Aug. 28-Sep. 3	August 19-25	August 4-10
September 4-10	Aug. 26-Sep. 1	August 11-17
September 11-17	September 2-8	August 18-24
} September 18-24	September 9-15 September 16-22	} August 25-31
Sep. 25-Oct. 1	September 23-29	September 1-7
October 2-21	Sep. 30-Oct. 9	September 8-27

Restoring the Context of Torah

> *"...As I exhorted you... instruct certain [men] not to teach any different doctrine, nor to pay attention to fables and endless genealogies that cause questions rather than the building up of God, which is by faith. And the goal of the instruction is love out of a pure heart and of a good conscience, and of faith undisguised, from which certain [men], having swerved [from these things], turned aside to fruitless discussion, wanting to be teachers of Torah, not understanding either the things they say, nor concerning what they [confidently] affirm. And we have known that the Torah is good, provided one uses it lawfully...." 1Timothy 1:3-8*

One of the major criticisms levied against the Messianic Jewish movement is that it allegedly causes believers in Yeshua to go back *"under the Law."*[1] Unfortunately, while much of our purported Torah observance is barely more than a superficial emulation of rabbinic Judaism, the accusation is not far from reality in some circumstances. Indeed, as the more

---

[1] cf. Romans 3:19, 1Corinthians 9:20, Galatians 3:23. Though not all Scriptural occurrences of "under the Law" connote "legalism" (as in Romans 6:14-15, Galatians 4:21 and 5:18), this is the inference of the criticism, nonetheless.

militant among our ranks swing to the extreme with their *versions* of Torah observance, it becomes the very legalism they vehemently swear to oppose. The practices and propaganda of many independents, fringe elements, and those in pseudo-Messianic[2] movements have also been cause for alarm within the larger Body of Messiah. Restoring the Torah to its proper context, therefore, ought to be of paramount concern for the Messianic Jewish movement.

While an exhaustive discussion of Torah observance—what it entails, who should do it, etc.—far exceeds the scope of this appendix, it will suffice to assert that it is incumbent upon Messianic Jews[3] within the context of Messianic Jewish communities to honor and embrace the covenant of Israel's national distinction, the Torah. It is no longer sufficient for each believer in Yeshua—Jew or Gentile—to approach Torah individualistically, hyper-spiritually, nonchalantly, legalistically, or any other way that is neither *"good"* nor *"lawful."* The keeping of the commands of Torah must be approached as ADONAI's means to an end—not the end itself—and that end is the restoration of the Jewish people to our covenantal calling as a light to the nations.[4]

As disciples of Messiah, we must fight the tendency to see only ourselves in the pages of Scripture, and instead look at the bigger picture of how ADONAI intends to restore humankind to Himself. While the Messiah Yeshua is the fullness of God's plan for global reconciliation, Israel continues to hold her central and

---

[2] So-called "Messianic" movements that are (a) birthed out of an accusatory or critical spirit toward Christianity, (b) have either a negative or neutral view toward Messianic Jews and the salvation of Jewish people, or (c) teach dubious doctrines that result in the appropriation of the Jew's unique identity among the nations.
[3] as well as the Gentiles who sojourn with us
[4] Deuteronomy 4:6ff, Isaiah 41:8, 42:1-6ff

irrevocable position in His purposes... and at the center of Israel's identity is ADONAI's Torah—both written and written on her heart—calling her to return to the covenant in order to complete the task she was first and forever set apart to do.

In our view, the restoration of the Torah begins with the simple premise that the written word should always be considered first in its original context, and last for its spiritual application.[5] The following list, though far from comprehensive, enumerates what we believe is a balanced beginning to a productive and fruitful approach to the Torah.

- ❖ Consider first the **national context** of a given passage of Torah. How is the passage speaking to the nation **of Israel** as a whole? What effect does obedience or disobedience have on the entire nation? Are the commands tied to Israel's occupation of the Land?

- ❖ Second, what impact should the passage have on **communal life within Israel**? How are neighbor-to-neighbor relationships affected? How does adherence to or ignorance of the passage build or destroy the life of a community?

- ❖ Third, how should an **individual living among a united, restored Israel** respond to the passage? What is his responsibility? How is he being practically instructed to think and behave?

- ❖ Fourth, consider how the instructions of a given passage translate to **community life in**

---

[5] This premise can certainly be extended to most, if not all, of Scripture.

dispersion. Can the commands be fully upheld? Partially? What should be our attitude toward commands that are unkeepable in our presently dispersed state? Can or should we be creative in our solutions to overcoming any obstacles to Torah-keeping?

❖ Fifth, what is our **individual responsibility** to the commands of Torah **while in dispersion**? How can we contribute to the building of our communities in spite of our dispersed condition? If community consensus is lacking, can we still honor the commands on an individual basis?

❖ Last, in light of all of the above, contemplate the **spiritual application** of the passage. How does the "doing" of the command affect us spiritually? How is the command fulfilled in Messiah? What is the best way for Messianic Jews—individually and communally—to understand and apply the passage? What, if any, is the broader spiritual application for all believers in Yeshua? How does it instruct, reprove, correct, or disciple us in righteousness?

By approaching the Torah in this manner, we will be able to consistently view it in its divinely given context: the constitutional covenant for a united, distinct nation of Israel—in the Land, under the direct headship of ADONAI our God. With this filter, we are better equipped to apply the Torah in our presently limited circumstances—dispersed among the nations, lacking in our communal identity—and begin to regain the perspective needed for Messianic Jews to enter into the fullness of our calling as covenantally faithful Israel.

About the Author

Kevin Geoffrey, born Kevin Geoffrey Berger, is the firstborn son of a first-generation American, non-religious, secular Jewish family. Ashamed of his heritage from childhood, Kevin deliberately attempted to hide his identity as a Jew. He spent his youth like most Jewish kids—essentially assimilated into American culture, embracing the things of the world and pursuing the things of the flesh.

At fifteen years of age, Kevin was diagnosed with Crohn's disease, a serious and incurable disorder of the digestive tract. After experiencing a sudden and apparently miraculous healing, Kevin's heart was opened to consider the possibility of something in which he had always been taught not to believe: the existence of God. A few years later, through various influential encounters and relationships, Kevin accepted Yeshua as Messiah and became what he then understood as a "born-again Christian."

Upon graduating from high school, Kevin rejected higher learning to half-heartedly pursue a career in music. With delusions of grandeur and his newfound identity as a "Christian," Kevin legally changed his name to Kevin Geoffrey, completing his assimilation from "Jew" to "Christian." When his ambition as a "rock star" ultimately failed to materialize, Kevin conceded defeat and entered Jacksonville University (Florida), where he graduated *magna cum laude*.

Throughout college, Kevin zealously studied the Scriptures. Seeking like-minded believers, he visited several Christian churches, but he was unable to find a place to call home. It was during this time that Kevin revealed his Jewish heritage to a close friend, who introduced him to the existence of the Messianic Jewish Movement.

In 1996, shortly before meeting his soon-to-be wife Esther, Kevin became part of a non-denominational Christian Fellowship where he was discipled in his faith, as well as in praise and worship ministry. Together, Kevin and Esther continued to learn about the Messianic Jewish Movement and became occasional attendees at the local Messianic congregation. Finally, after their Christian Fellowship suffered a devastating split, Kevin was able to fully embrace his call as a Messianic Jew and was restored to his Jewish heritage.

Today, Kevin is a strong advocate for the restoration of Jewish believers in Yeshua to their distinct calling and identity as the remnant of Israel. Kevin is the founder of Perfect Word Ministries, a Messianic Jewish equipping ministry, which he currently serves as President and Director. He is the author of the *Messianic Devotional* and *The Messianic Life* series, and is a regular contributor to *Jewish Voice Today* magazine. In 2006, Kevin was licensed as a Messianic Jewish Teacher by the IAMCS (International Alliance of Messianic Congregations and Synagogues), and ordained in 2008 by JVMI (Jewish Voice Ministries International). Kevin has taught in live seminars and conferences throughout the United States, as well as multiple Messianic congregations and synagogues. He has also served in congregational leadership, and as an anointed worship leader both in congregations and in regional and national Messianic conferences. Kevin resides in Phoenix, Arizona with his wife Esther and their three beautiful sons, Isaac, Josiah and Hosea.

A Messianic Jewish Equipping Ministry

Other Resources Available from Perfect Word

Messianic Jewish Teachings

❖ *The Messianic Life* discipleship publication

❖ *Preparing The Way* monthly audio teachings

Devotional Books

❖ Messianic Daily Devotional

❖ Messianic Mo'adiym Devotional

❖ Messianic Torah Devotional

The Messianic Life Series
Small Group & Personal Study Resources

❖ Being A Disciple of Messiah

❖ The Fruit of the Spirit (forthcoming)

www.PerfectWordMinistries.com

**Calling the Body of Messiah to maturity
by teaching the simple application of Scripture
for a radically changed life in Yeshua**

CPSIA information can be obtained at www.ICGtesting.com
Printed in the USA
LVOW041048110812

293660LV00005B/13/P